"Biz"

Shorts

Shorts

35 Wisdoms for Your Business Life's Strife

(With Minis)

Derrick Watts

	SHORT / BIZ TOPIC	PAGE

	SHORT / BIZ TOPIC	PAGE

Typically, business books are written by super intelligent people who consult with companies around the world or books are written by scholars who have multiple acronyms listed after their names. They use ten-dollar words to describe their content and devise some unique terminology all to describe solutions to the same business situations you already know. Additionally, the business books of today drill-down on isolated issues in the business environment offering over-analysis on just a few business conditions. Often the result finds the author not connecting with the reader and finds the reader left wanting for a little more fulfillment from digesting the reading. What about a book for the normal business person addressing a variety of everyday problems and opportunities in an entertaining way? Here it is: Biz Shorts.

Biz Shorts are a series of short stories and messages designed to enhance interpersonal skills and address the intangibles of business situations faced by business leaders, managers and other decision makers. The format allows for nugget-sized stirring messages woven through an entertaining story or situation. The result is the reader is enriched in an enjoying fashion. Some Biz Shorts deal with a business concept, while others deal with personal behavioral attributes.

Biz Shorts is my second book and follow up to "Shorts", 52 Devotionals for Your Weekly Life's Strife (ISBN: 978-1-62510-477-9), a series of Christian devotionals. I love to read devotionals. Their short messages carry a powerful result enriching the soul and bringing the reader closer to God. By contrast, Biz Shorts carries the same short and enriching format into the business arena. I have direct or indirect experience with all my shorts, which allows me to authentically convey a real message and solution. I have work experience on three continents. My responsibilities have covered a number of areas, such as process improvement, financial analysis, due-diligence, post due-diligence, sales, operations, customer service and management. I've worked for fortune 500 companies, been a co-founder of a start up company and I am green-belt certified (a Six-Sigma classification). I've worked for a large company with the lowest national market share and worked for a smaller company with the highest national market share so my experiences carry an appropriate breadth and depth in the business world.

I wrote this book for three reasons:

1) Time is very short, yet we all need to continue enriching our minds and improving ourselves.

2) I wanted to share my experiences and possibly help others.

3) The business genre in print needs a broader, lighter and more effective approach to connect with readers.

Biz Shorts is the perfect book for students, young professionals, seasoned business veterans and even for folks not engaged in generating revenue or producing a profit...essentially everyone!

I do have several people to thank: my sons Trevor, Shane & Andrew - they are in my mind, especially when writing short stories, in hopes these bits of enrichment will be learning points for them one day; my wife, Kim, who is the "rock" of our family, pretty special, and my personal editor; my parents for raising me in an environment allowing me to have a decent education; Michele Howard, former boss; Troy Hartman, my friend, business partner and boss; finally, to all the wonderful folks at ExamOne...you rock!

Please enjoy my shorts and feel free to access my blog website at www.devotionalshorts.com.

Derrick Watts, MBA

ONE

THE EMPEROR'S NEW CLOTHES:
Courage

All the glasses were raised as dad made a toast, "To Mitch, congratulations for becoming the top banana out of the whole bunch. We wish you the brightest future and go confidently in pursuit of your dreams."

Everyone clanked their glasses and smiled with approval. The family and a few close friends had gathered to celebrate Mitch's promotion as he was the youngest in the firm to reach the director level. He would now join a peer group to collaborate on business events, but, at the same time, indirectly compete against each other for the next level of achieving "partner" status in the firm. Everyone went around the table to add some encouraging words or to offer a gift gesturing the sentiment of congratulations. One gift was an engraved paper weight, while another was a business card holder and all of them seemed to be straight from the Sharper Image catalog.

It was now grandpa's turn and everyone gave attention to observe respect for the patriarch of the family. Grandpa's health had recently deteriorated to the point of physically needing a walker and speaking with a slowing and slurred speech. Grandpa pulled a book out of a used and crinkled brown paper sack. The book was the Emperor's New Clothes, a popular fable for kids. Collectively, everyone's smiles faded and they looked at each other with concern for grandpa as this gift was for kids and certainly not for business.

Grandpa broke the silence clearing his voice and gently spoke, "That's the story of the narcissistic emperor where two swindlers tailored him a suit of clothes for a special public parade...remember?" The family nodded in acknowledgement to grandpa, but then looked at each other as if Grandpa was experiencing dementia. Grandpa continued, "The tailors conned everyone by saying that the fabric was invisible to anyone who was unfit for their position, so everyone was afraid to say something for fear of exposing themselves as being unfit. They kept up the pretenses even during the parade until a boy, who was too young to understand pretenses, pointed out the emperor was wearing nothin."

Mitch interrupted Grandpa with intentions to save his embarrassment and replied, "why thanks Gpa...I remember you telling me that story growing up." Mitch looked at his wife and then his dad with concern. As the party wound down, Mitch helped dad take grandpa to the car.

On the way home, Mitch was mostly pre-occupied with grandpa's sudden appearance of mental decay. He recounted with his wife that grandpa had been very active in Mitch's life, but now Mitch was suddenly very embarrassed for grandpa and equally felt sorry that a great man would mentally fall in this manner. This was the man who taught Mitch to fish, throw a baseball properly and even helped teach him to drive. Mitch could not understand what logical reason why grandpa would give him that book as opposed to a business nick-knack. Mitch rationalized that grandpa maybe grabbed that book by mistake, yet grandpa spoke at about the book at the party. Then Mitch thought maybe grandpa just didn't have anything else to give, but grandpa had plenty of resources so that wasn't true either.

By time Mitch's family reached home it was late. As Mitch's wife helped get their children ready for bed, Mitch rubbed the book with his hands trying to discern whether his grandpa was becoming unbalanced in his thinking. After a few pondering moments, Mitch thought he could at least put the book to some use by reading it to his children. Just then he opened the book and on the inside cover and the following message starred him in the face: *Mitchie - I have long felt that you would reach a successful point in your life. Hopefully, this is the first in many to come. It is now important then ever that you become aware of the meaning of this fable. You see, most likely your peers will "keep with the pretenses" and let the emperor walk around without clothes. They will do this in an attempt to increase favor with the emperor. Mitchie, it will be important for you to have the courage to call out invisible clothes when you see them dressed on your emperor. You will stand alone holding true to your principles and the values of your company. You will have to balance how you can manage a relationship with those who keep the pretenses and with those*

who need you, alone, to point out the truth. I love you and pray
for your courage. Congratulations, Grandpa.

Upon Mitch reading these words, tears raced down his face.
Mitch's wife came down the stairs and noticed his
crying condition. "What happened?", she shrieked excitedly.

Mitch wiped some tears, gave a relieving smile and said, "I
should have known, he's ok." Mitch's wife looked confused but
said nothing. Mitch continued, "Unlike all those Sharper Image
tokens, gpa gave the best gift anyone could ever receive!"

Mitch handed her the book opened to the message.

Reflection:

> 1) How are your vocational pretenses compared to
> your peers?
>
> 2) Do you know the principles and values established
> in your vocation?
>
> 3) What would keep you from being courageous in
> your vocation?

TWO

THE CASE OF THE BROKEN YO-YO:
Know the "When" for Strategy and Tactics

Tony recruited Doug to work for him years ago when company performance was at an unprecedented run in the market place. However, now results were on a plateau and Tony sensed the organization needed to move in a different direction to stay in front of the competitors. Tony held multiple conceptual sessions where he wanted the "minds" in the organization to think differently. He held working meetings where the management team set the strategies and tactics in place to achieve Tony's new directional objective. Doug was a key player with the company transition; however, the transition was moving slower then expected. Tony invited Doug to lunch to recap the most recent progress with the strategy and tactics. After they ate and reviewed some information, Tony pulled a small box out of his sports jacket and slid it across the table towards Doug. Doug was pleasantly surprised and had no idea what gift was concealed inside.

"What in the world is this?" Doug asked excitedly. Tony smiled and, without speaking, extended his hand out to gesture to open the box. As Doug opened the box, his face gave way to a perplexing smile as the gift was a yo-yo. Doug looked in wonder to Tony and pulled the yo-yo out of the box. The yo-yo actually appeared to be broken with its string unwound and intentionally knotted so that it could not be wound. Now Tony was known and admired for his unique wit, so Doug tried to solve this puzzle without asking Tony. After a few moments of silent smiling stares, Doug gave up. Doug said, "Well thank you...but I don't get it."

Tony replied, "It's symbolism for the situation we're in operationally."

Doug raised his eyebrows in confusion and replied, "I don't understand what a broken yo-yo has to do with our organizational changes."

Tony raised his hand with his pointer finger in the way as if to signal to Doug to wait on the questioning. Tony replied, "Our tactics are not congruent with our strategy and that is part of the reason our organizational change is struggling."

Doug replied, "Right, we just covered some of our tactical challenges, but I don't know what that has to do with this broken yo-yo."

Tony pinched the bridge of his nose as if to find the right words and replied, "Our management team needs to better understand when to spend time with forming strategy and executing tactics. When properly operated the yo-yo will unwind down and rewind up given the specific movements of the hand. Our management team must think strategy when the yo-yo is in the 'up' rewind position and must disseminate tactics when unwound in the 'down' position. Our problem is our management team is like this broken yo-yo where it is constantly unwound in the tactical position."

The analogy clicked with Doug and he eagerly responded, "Yes, I sense that every time we discuss a high-level concept the team can't help but get caught up in the details of a solution. Do you think that is part of our transitional problem towards our objective?"

Tony nodded and replied, "Our team jumps right to the detail of a concept without working through the strategic positioning to our objective. Our key people are the yo-yo and they need to know when to be wound in strategy and unwound in tactics. Until they understand the strategic approach we will take to reach our goal, how can we incorporate tactical tools to execute our strategy?" Doug nodded with acceptance, sat silent and let the analogy sink into his mind. Tony continued, "Doug, you are my biggest yo-yo and I need you to make sure all our other yo-yos are not broken like this one." They both laughed at the humor in the analogy as Doug picked up the yo-yo to inspect it.

Doug smiled and wittingly replied, "Yo...I am your yo-yo guy and we'll be doing 'walk-the-dog' and other strategy tricks before you know it!"

Reflection:

1) Do you understand the place and time to operate with strategy or in tactics in your vocation?

2) Does your strategy reconcile to your goal?

3) Do your tactics support your strategy?

THREE

THE JANITOR:
Everyone has an Important Role

The interview process had whittled down between two candidates. Each candidate was brought in for a series of "one-on-ones" with several members from the management team. One candidate, David, connected well with some key people who would make the decision to hire. David asked all the right questions and sensed positive vibes with much of the non-verbal interaction. David was convinced that he would be chosen.

A week elapsed and there was no word from the company. Confused and eager, David contacted his Human Resources contact in search of an update. The next day he received a letter thanking him for his interest, but the company had made a decision with the other candidate. David was shocked and replayed in his head the events of the interview process. This frustrated him as he felt he was lead to believe that he was the obvious choice. In frustration he reached out to a key decision maker asking for some feedback. The decision maker agreed with David that he would have been a good fit; however, stated that the group's decision was trumped. David concluded this final decision could only come from the president of the company so, with courage, David asked the president's assistant for a call. Kathy, the president agreed to a short follow up discussion with David.

After exchanging a few pleasantries, David acknowledged Kathy's busy schedule and simply recapped the disparity between his positive interview experiences and the decision. Kathy thanked him for his interest in the company and added, "Durwin is the name of our janitor."

David didn't understand what Kathy said and replied, "Were you speaking to me? I don't understand."

Kathy expounded, "David, our company requires every single employee to push or pull in the same direction for us to achieve any level of success. Although we have different responsibilities, our functions are critical to each other. You might say our sum total is greater than our individual parts. No one is less important including our janitor and, again, his name is Durwin. David, when we visited I asked you if you knew your janitor in your existing job...do you remember what you told me?"

The phone line was silent as David was trying to remember the details of his conversation with Kathy. David eventually replied, "I don't think I remember, but I know I but I am sure the janitors at my existing employment do fine."

Kathy responded, "Ok, David that may be fine but when we talked, you referred to your cleaning service as a commodity and joked you would replace them if the trash cans were not emptied."

David said, "I understand everyone in an organization is important, but surely my talents supersede any sentiment towards a janitor."

Kathy replied, "David, you are a talented person and I am speaking to you in hopes to make you more valuable to any organization you represent. In your career, you will meet many people. They are all significant and deserve your attention and care. Even if all you do is smile and say hello to your cleaning service...you will be a company conduit connecting them with the greater company purpose."

David responded, "I think I understand now, thank you for your time, and I will never forget this lesson." Tomorrow, I will start learning more about people and make my organization better.

Kathy said, "Wonderful, the moment you do that you will also make yourself better. Good luck."

Reflection:

1) Can you remember a time when something seemingly insignificant to you made a big difference with something you wanted?

2) How can someone add value when he/she is not tied to producing revenue and/or profit?

3) How can you be more inclusive in your vocation?

FOUR

NO FAIR! THE SMART PHONE:
Equal Verses Fair

"Make a wish," mom suggested excitedly. Shane blew out all eleven candles on his cake. It had been a great birthday as Shane had scored on many of the presents he wanted. Everyone started picking up the wrapping paper and Shane started to consolidate his presents into one manageable pile. Just then a telephone started to ring. Shane didn't pay attention and continued to separate the wrapping paper from gifts. The phone kept ringing so Shane took notice in an innocent yet, inquisitive way.

Mom broke her stone-faced composure and asked, "Shane, where do you think that noise is coming from?" Shane shrugged his shoulders as he didn't know, but hopped to his feet to begin a helpful search. Shane's search took him to the crease between the couch cushions. He slithered in his hand and pulled out a ringing smart-phone. Shane answered and on the other end was mom laughing, "Happy birthday!" Shane was very excited at the prospect of giving up his single-function cell phone for the unlimited features of a smart phone. He jumped up and down and rushed over to mom to offer an approving hug.

The commotion caught the attention of Shane's younger brother, Andrew. Andrew took an inventory of the situation and decided he didn't like the outcome. Andrew pierced the spirit of the celebration by offering a loud shriek of disapproval. "No fair!," Andrew bellowed. As the attention in the room turned to Andrew, he welled up with tears and stomped off to his room. Mom followed Andrew to console her pouty, baby boy.

It was getting late, so the family members left one by one leaving the final touches of cleaning to dad and Shane. Shane retired to his room to enjoy his birthday gifts and dad decided to let mom handle the "Andrew situation." After awhile mom came out smiling and plopped down next to dad who was watching television.

With an idea already in mind, dad went ahead and asked, "What's up with Andrew?"

Mom replied, "He thought it was unfair for Shane to have a phone without him having one."

Dad laughed and replied, "He's in Kindergarten...who's he going to call...Big Bird?"

Mom chuckled and said, "six year-olds don't understand the difference between equal verses fair."

Dad asked, "What did you tell him?"

Mom replied, "He kept repeating into his pillow, sniffling of course, "no fair, no fair' so I got out his iPod touch and dangled it in front of him. He held in protective fashion like I was going to take it, so I told him that you and I loved him and his brother equally, yet since they are two separate people we needed to treat them differently but fairly."

Dad interrupted, "So you compared his iPod touch to Shane's smart phone and called it equal?"

Mom shook her finger back and forth as if to correct dad and said, "No, Shane is eleven and Andrew is six so they cannot be treated equally. Our job is to ensure they are treated proportionately fair in our family."

Dad nodded in agreement and replied, "I get it now. We got Andrew an IPod touch and that is fairly commensurate to Shane's smart phone given Andrew's age."

Mom smiled and answered, "Yes, very good and I gave other examples too like Andrew's machine pitch baseball is age proportionately fair to Shane's real baseball team."

Impressed dad replied, "Sounds like you did well to diffuse the situation...do you think Andrew bought it?"

Mom snickered and repeated, "It's hard for a six year-old to understand the difference between equal and fair."

Dad and mom watched some television and a work situation snuck into dad's mind. Dad said, "you know, it's not just six year-olds who don't understand the difference between equal and fair." Mom looked at dad perplexed. Dad rolled his eyes, tilted his head backwards and sighed, "At work, corporate came down with this cost-cutting edict where we have to drop our operational costs by ten percent across the board. This really sucks because our division is meeting our numbers, but since the core business is down then everyone has to take their 'fair share'."

Mom inserted, "Unbelievable, They call this fair when really it's equal just as Andrew called no fair when he really meant equal."

Dad added, "And with adults even."

Mom replied, "So let me get this straight...you are meeting your budget but you have to cut the same percent for fairness sake as others because other businesses are falling short?"

Dad nodded and replied sarcastically, "Yep, so if this household was corporate, we would be getting our six year-old a smart phone so that all is equal...across the board so to speak."

Mom shook her head and asked, "So, how are you handling it?"

Dad grimaced and replied, "Well not very well, but we are trying to balance being a good corporate citizen with inserting the notion that cuts should be proportioned to a factor of our size coupled with our success. That way we can contribute to the greater good with some cuts, while still maintaining focus on execution in our own division. Their concept of equal can damage our business, while really not helping corporate. Conversely, if we can win our concept of fairness then we can promote continued health in both our businesses"

Mom offered, "Maybe I should go teach them the difference between equal verses fair?"

Dad smirked and replied, "Yeah, but I think you'd get the same reaction out of corporate as you got out of our six year-old."

Reflection:

> 1) Can you identify areas in your vocation where the equal vs. fair problem exists?
>
> 2) Is there a way you can adjust things proportionately so that "equal" transitions to "fair"?
>
> 3) Can you explain to others that the concept of fairness is healthier for your business?

FIVE

UNCLE WAYNE'S COWS:
Leveraging Fixed Costs

Wes bounced down the stairs and announced to dad he would be needing help with homework. He then made a casual bypass through the kitchen for a snack before plopping down on the couch beside dad.

Wes asked, "Dad, I need to write a paragraph for school about the difference between fixed and variable costs...do you have an example I could use?"

Dad smiled with appreciation, turned the television off and shifted his eyes upward in thought. With a little hum he responded, "Actually Uncle Wayne's cows come to mind." Wes' face scrunched as if to show a lack of approval and said, "Dad, I don't want to write about cows. What do they have to do with costs anyway."

With a slight sarcasm dad replied, "Uncle Wayne's cows weren't pets...they were part of his business as a farmer which directly involved both fixed and variable costs. Do you want my help or not?" Reluctantly, Wes nodded yes. Dad continued, "Uncle Wayne operated a cow-calf operation, which means he raised calves and sold them into the market place when they matured. There are a number of fixed costs associated with raising cows, such as the property, all the fencing and the labor.

Wes asked, "Labor...you mean workers?" Dad replied, "Yes, remember there were two workers named Clayton and Jim who helped Uncle Wayne on the farm." Wes tapped his memory and acknowledged with a nod yes. Dad continued, "So those costs are considered as direct. Now the variable costs represent things such as the feed provided to the cows. The feed amount and cost varied with the volume and size of the cattle. This is really a usable definition of variable cost as the cost is contingent on specific and multiple factors."

Wes jotted some random things on a piece of paper and replied, "Ok, so the fixed cost is the barn and other things used in keeping the cows and variable costs change depending on how many and how big the cows are."

Dad smiled and said, "That's perfect the way you said it. Just remember that when you write your paragraph?"

Wes nodded and hopped off the couch. As he scurried up the stairs, he stopped mid-way and asked, "Did Uncle Wayne make a lot of money with his cows?"

Dad, looked back at Wes and replied, "Actually, yes but it wasn't easy. The variable cost feed was very expensive and represented about fifty percent of the total cost of each cow. However, do you want to hear Uncle Wayne's secret for cow success?" Wes turned around on the stairs and raced back to the couch." Dad continued, "Uncle Wayne leveraged his fixed costs and reduced his variable costs by supplementing his cow-calf operation with another form of cattle raising known as the stock method. This method purchased adolescent cows in the spring and used the natural pasture grass and hay to feed them until they were ready for sale in the fall. The pasture, the pasture grass and the hay were already costs involved in the operation of Uncle Wayne's farm. He leveraged these fixed costs for another purpose to make money that was a complement to his traditional cattle business.

Wes responded, "So Uncle Wayne increased his margin on the two types of cow operations he ran?"

Dad replied, "Yes, it makes "udder" sense...doesn't it?"

Wes replied, "Dad, you are good with helping me with my homework, but bad at telling jokes!"

Dad replied, "Oh ya, well why don't you "mooove" on upstairs!"

Reflection:

1) Do you understand the difference between a fixed and variable cost?

2) Can you identify an opportunity in your vocation to move a fixed cost to a variable cost?

3) How is it possible to leverage a fixed cost in your organization?

SIX

TEXAS HOLD 'EM:
Riding the Fence of Inaction

Greg wasn't a big card player, but he agreed to attend his neighbor's Texas hold 'em party. Amazingly, Greg was one of only five players left who had survived three tables of competitors going bust in the variation of the poker game. Just like other poker games, Texas hold 'em strategy is rooted in making a competitive hand out of random cards and bluffing competitors. However, Greg took a different path to reach the final table. If his hand didn't have face cards or multiples of same numbered cards, he would fold and not play. Additionally, he typically folded, conservatively, before the final rounds of betting larger money.

This strategy appeared to work as it got him to the final table; however, now he faced a significant problem. His chip resources had dwindled so much that he was barely able to ante-up on a small-blind. Greg peeked under the cards. One was the six of hearts and the other was the nine of Diamonds. Greg tried not to show his dislike for the cards but did twist his head attempting to relieve stress through popping his neck joint. As the bidding was going around the table he wished that he would not have folded on the last hand but wished he could fold on this hand. He could not fold now because he was the small-blind and his ten dollars of chips would be wasted if he didn't continue to play.

Greg's neighbor whispered over his shoulder that he should bet "all-in" to have a chance to play in the next round. Greg was not excited about the advice, because he didn't have anything going with the two cards he had. He decided to fold and kiss away his small-blind money, but he would survive to play another round. In the next hand, Greg was now the large-blind and had to ante-up with twenty dollars in chips, which left him little to bet the hand. Greg's two cards were playable as he received a pair of fours. Greg decided to take his neighbor's advice and he bet "all-in". The remaining players had varying amounts of chips, but all of them had a healthy surplus over what Greg had.

The other players never saw Greg as a threat and now were ready to eliminate him out of the way. They all matched his bid and raised it. The other three cards were dealt revealing a jack of spades, a four of hearts and the ten of diamonds. Greg had a three of a kind now and that would be hard to beat. Unfortunately, Greg didn't have additional chips to bet. The other players might have shown discernment with a strategic bluff earlier, but now they were ready to call Greg's hand. It turns out that someone else had a full house and won the kitty, which meant Greg's run had come to an end. Afterwards, Greg regretted using his card strategy and wished he had made different decisions.

Although Greg made it to the final table of players, he was in no condition to compete. He never won a hand so he only had the illusion of success by making it to the final table. He was actually suffering from an idiom known as "death by a thousand cuts". Doing nothing always seems to be the safe decision at the time, but often inaction leads to paving the path of earning unwanted, regretful consequences. The reality is that Greg's inaction prevented him from competing.

In business, riding the fence on decisions can project the same illusion of perceived success that Greg experienced. Will Rogers once said, "even if you are on the right track, you'll get run over if you just sit there." The things people don't do in their business far outweigh the things people do. It could be that the inertia surrounding transitioning organized thoughts into specific decisions is simply too great. Fear of making the wrong decision, conflict avoidance or the effort of a decision perceptively outweighing the the result are all examples of inertia inaction. Probably, the biggest ride-the-fence offense is a lack of engagement with the issue. The person of inaction may be responsible for the decision in question, but for whatever reason is not personally connected with the circumstances. Therefore, the lack of engagement actually promotes the person of inaction to remain idle. Our card player, Greg, didn't have an engagement with Texas Hold 'em, so that enabled him to move through the game with inaction. This type of behavior can be addictive too. If the person of inaction sees no immediate adverse impact to inaction then that becomes an enabler for future inaction. The result is an inactive leader can foster the growth of mild resentment with downstream employees, because they are the ones who have to directly deal with the consequences of inaction.

Commentary:

There are three keys to decision making that keeps a leader from riding the fence of inaction:

1) The biggest key is to increase the engagement level with the circumstances surrounding the potential decision. As a leader, you need to renew yourself with the backdrop surrounding the situation. A connection is made when you can understand the interconnectedness between the current situation and the pending decision.

2) Another key is increasing discernment through weighing the possible outcomes of the pending decision. This can be achieved through creating a list of pros and cons for each potential decision avenue or consulting with others who face similar circumstantial challenges.

3) Finally, get off the fence, make a confident decision and make down-line adjustments if necessary.

There are no guarantees to a right decision as hindsight is always 20/20. Mistakes can be corrected and should be viewed as valuable learning experiences from the decision making process. On the other hand, no one can reclaim the time lost nor reduce the frustration spawned through the delay of learning nothing through inaction. Therefore, don't second guess yourself and rejoice that you didn't regret folding your playing hand through inaction.

Reflection:

1) Can you think of some consequences of inaction with your vocation?

2) Are you riding the fence on a decision?

3) Are you connected with the three keys when making a decision?

SEVEN

THE FORGOTTEN COWBOY:
Primacy & Recency

Little Eric was eager to help Ray feed the animals. Eric's dad,
Ben, had really played up the experience. Ray was a long-time
friend of the family who had sold his successful business. He
had purchased acreage and liked to play farmer just as a
hobby toying with maintaining livestock. Actually, Ray had
several animal types ranging from cows and horses to even
lamas. Eric and Ben met Ray out at his barn. Ray already had
his work truck loaded with the necessary feed for the variety of
animals he had. Eric hopped up in the middle seat next to Ray
with Ben slipping in behind him shutting the door and tapping
twice on the side of the door indicating they were all ready to
go. Ray pulled out of the barnyard and headed towards the
pasture entrance. As they drove Ray told some stories about
some of the funny things his animals have done. Ray was
entertaining and a bit of a character with his personality.

As the driving continued, Ray turned his attention to Eric. "Hey
bud," Ray said has he tapped Eric's shoulder, "You ready to be
a cowboy today?" Eric acted a little shy, but nodded yes as he
leaned into his dad's arms. Ray asked Eric, " Hey, us three
cowboys are sitting here in the truck...do you know who the

smartest cowboy is?" Eric shrugged his shoulders indicating he didn't know and Ben was now listening intently waiting for the punch line. Ray continued, "Well, it's not your dad as he's the one that has to get out of the truck constantly opening and closing the pasture gates." Eric looked at his dad, pointed and snickered. Eric turned back and looked at Ray. Excitedly Ray said, "Don't look at me...I'm not the smartest cowboy as I have to load the feed and drive the truck."

So now confused, Eric asked, "Wait, so who is the smartest cowboy?"

Ray's face showed a big grin and answered, "Why, the smartest cowboy is the guy that sits in the middle. He doesn't have to drive the truck or get out and open gates. All that guy has to do is sit there and enjoy life!" As Ray finished his sentence he wiggled his pointer finger towards Eric tickling him in the ribs.

Eric laughed and remarked, "I don't have a job so I sound more like the forgotten cowboy instead of the smartest cowboy."

Ben smiled patting Eric on the shoulder and responded, "Yeah, you're just like a business presentation...everyone remembers the first part and the last part of a presentation, but everyone forgets the middle part." Ray bellowed with laughter identifying with the statement." Eric didn't understand but was pleased that he created such fun so he joined in with the laughter." Paying homage to Ray's business acumen, Ben asked, "What's up with people and that phenomenon anyway?"

Ray tilted his head as if he was looking on the ceiling of the truck and replied, "I think the concept is called primacy and recency. People psychologically remember better the first and the most recent thing they hear or see. I guess they get lost or forget what's in the middle."

Ben pondered and a little and then broke into perspective regarding his business. Ben said, "You know, this might be one of our problems with our sales team." The conversation was above Eric's head but he was actively listening. Ben continued, "We hired a marketing firm to spice up the PowerPoint presentation for our sales people. The presentation gives our company history in the primacy, gives our sales pitch in the middle and follows with the industry update in the recency."

Ray nodded and confirmed, "Yeah, you probably need to change that workflow and get back to catching peoples attention." Ray continued, "In my business, we always liked to get them excited up front and use the end to close a sales deal still while the excitement of the emotion was high." Ben acknowledged with a big nod. Just then the truck pulled up to the pasture gate.

Eric blurted out, "Hey Recency...Primacy needs you to open the gate!" Both Ben and Ray looked at each other in disbelief that Eric could remotely follow the conversation while being sassy at the same time. They both broke out into heavy laughter. Eric laughed too.

After wiping tears of laughter from his eyes, Ben said, "So much for the forgotten cowboy."

Ray quipped, "No, I told you he was the smartest cowboy!"

Reflection:

> 1) Do customers get lost with the informational pitches in your vocation?
>
> 2) Is there a distinct strategy to present your products and/or services?
>
> 3) How could customers be more "wowed" when learning about your products and/or services?

EIGHT

THE HARLEY TATTOO:

Brand Recognition, Identity & Loyalty

Driving down the road, Tyler noticed a McDonalds' sign and recalled a discussion he had in class at school. Tyler decided to share his knowledge with dad. "Hey dad", Tyler asked inquisitively, "Do you know the most recognized symbol of any business in America?" Dad noticed Tyler analyzing the sign so he figured Tyler was referring to McDonalds.

Dad replied, "Do you mean the recognition of a company logo?" Tyler nodded impatiently hoping to beat dad to the answer of his own question. Dad played along and replied, "uh, how about Nike?"

Dad's guess surprised Tyler, so he replied, "Good guess, but my teacher says that is the second most recognizable logo...do you know the first?" Dad wanted to let Tyler have his fun so he continued driving while shrugging his shoulders as if he didn't know. Triumphantly Tyler boasted, "The golden arches dad...Mickey D's." (1)

Dad agreed with a head nod and replied, "So McDonalds is the most recognizable brand with Nike as the second." So now dad posed a question, "What is the one word you immediately think of when you hear McDonalds?"

Tyler bit on his tongue for a second and responded, "Even though I don't eat them now, I think of a happy meal."

Dad nodded his head with approval and said, "yeah, I agree as I think of kids and cheap food."

Tyler asked, "So what is a brand supposed to do?" Dad thought for a moment and replied, "Well son, I am not in marketing but I think a brand helps a company provide messaging that helps define the company in a way identified by customers." Tyler seemed confused so dad continued, "Brands are symbols that associate useful value with what the company believes in. Let's use your mom as an example. Since her family is from Germany, she loves what kind of car?"

Tyler quickly offered, "BMW."

Dad smiled and said, "Exactly right and what is the one word mom often uses to describe a BMW?"

Again, Tyler immediately replied, "Performance!"

Dad answered, "Absolutely." Next dad asked, "What is the other German car and the one word that mom uses to describe it?"

Tyler had to think just a moment, but then blurted, "Mercedes and engineering."

Dad smiled and said, "Very good. Look at what those brands have messaged to your mom and now to you. We recognize those brands and immediately identify the company's value proposition.

Tyler was nodding and added, "So for me McDonalds won the brand recognition battle because of messaging to kids with offering happy meals and toys."

During this time, a biker on a Harley Davidson motorcycle rumbled by in the passing lane. By this time dad was really impressed and said, "Son, you are cranking full power on the concept so let's go one step further."

Tyler asked, "What else is associated with branding?"

Dad responded, "A few things but specifically loyalty; and it has something to do with the motorcycle that just passed us." Dad continued, "What brand was that motorcycle?"

Tyler replied, "I saw the wings in the logo and, by the way it sounded, it had to be a Harley."

Dad agreed with a nod and asked, "Good, you recognized a brand. Why do you think the Harley Davidson brand might possess great loyalty with customers?" Tyler thought about it and just couldn't come up with anything of substance. Dad decided to give a hint and asked, "Remember the Harley biker guy standing in line at the store earlier today?" Tyler nodded yes. Dad asked, "What was really big on his arm?"

Quickly Tyler answered, "A Harley tattoo." Dad nodded and added, "Exactly, how many customers get a tattoo for a company's product?" Tyler thought about it and then shrugged his shoulders as if he didn't know. Then dad asked, "Do you see anyone with the golden arches tattooed on his arm?"

Tyler laughed and replied, No, I don't think so."

Smiling dad added, "Why not?"

Tyler replied, "Because you said it is cheap food for kids so that's not a cool enough identity."

Dad smiled and said, "Maybe...who knows, but I don't think many people even get BMW tattoos and remember that their brand identity is cool."

Tyler thought about it and said, okay so McDonalds has strong brand recognition, BMW has a strong brand identity, but a product tattoo represents a strong brand loyalty."

Dad patted Tyler on the back and laughed, "I think you are ready for a perfect score whenever you take a marketing class. Just remember that all these companies are successful, but Harley was able to create a special value connection with its customer base.

Tyler asked, "What would Harley's brand identity be?"

Dad thought for a moment and then gave a description. Dad said, "Remember what I do. I wear a dress shirt and slacks to work and push paper around, I have calls and I attend meetings. Look at that Harley rider off in the distance." Tyler stretched up to make sure he could see the whole motorcycle over the car dashboard. After a moment dad asked, "So my work situation can be described as confining...what does that Harley biker look like?"

Tyler nodded and guessed, "He looks free." In amazement dad responded, "Yes, freedom...that is exactly as I was thinking. Somehow Harley was able to humanize the brand getting an emotional connection between the product and a desired way of life from the customer. The coolest companies win the brand recognition, identity and the loyalty game when it comes to marketing." Dad ended, "So now you can take back to your teacher that you know brand recognition can stretch further into brand identity and loyalty. However, just do me one favor."

Tyler asked, "What dad?"

Dad smiled and replied, "When explaining about brand loyalty, just tell your teacher and leave the tattoo off your arm!"

Reflection:

> 1) Is the brand recognition and identity obvious in your vocation?
>
> 2) How could you improve your brand loyalty?
>
> 3) With all the marketing messages, how are your discerning qualities between brands?

(1) http://www.rankingthebrands.com/The-Brand-Rankings.aspx – note, McDonalds ranked 6th in 2012 and was used in-part for illustrative purposes and based on a real conversation with my son.

NINE

MARSHMALLOWS & TOOTHPICKS:

Bad Group Decisions

The teacher looked at his watch and announced, "Thirty seconds." The teams echoed with chatter as they placed their finishing touches on their constructed towers. The object was for a group to build the tallest free-standing structure made from only marshmallows and toothpicks.

The teacher barked, "Ok...hands away from your creations. Now we'll see some results of your planning, engineering and teamwork skills." The teacher extended the measuring tape from the container and slapped it on the table for an audio effect. "Remember," the teacher said, "the tower has stay standing while I measure from the table to the highest point." The teacher approached the first tower, which measured twenty-five inches. The group congratulated each other and waited patiently to hear the results from their competitors. The second group measured just shy of twenty-three inches so group one was still in the lead. Just at that moment, the tower of the last group fell, which spurred some collective gasps from the group.

One person from the fallen group protested, "You should have measured us first!"

As the teacher began measuring the fallen tower, the teacher quipped, "Ah, remember the structure has to stay standing." The teacher measured and reported, "twelve inches...group number one wins."

Another frustrated member from the third group announced, "I disagreed with the design from the start."

A second group member replied, "Well I did too."

Another member argued back, "Wait a minute...although I suggested the design, I was not sold on it, but you both agreed to it."

All three students started incoherently debating. The teacher interrupted by raising his hand in a pausing motion and clearing his throat. As the group quieted the teacher commented, "What you are experiencing is a classic case of the phenomenon known as the Abilene Paradox."

Two students from the fallen group simultaneously asked, "The Abilene what?"

The teacher giggled and replied, "Let's take our seats and I'll break it down for you."

Once students returned to their seats, the teacher sat on the edge of the desk and started describing the scene for the Abilene Paradox. The teacher said, "Ok, a husband, wife and in-laws are back in the 1950's during a hot Sunday summer day in the rural Texas outside of Abilene. This is before air-conditioning, paved roads and interstate highways. The four are sitting on their porch seeking a shady refuge from the sun. Assuming all are bored, the father in-law suggests they load into the car and travel fifty miles into Abilene to eat at the diner. Without objection they travel in a hot car down dusty roads, reaching a crowded diner and experiencing less than average food. Once back at home, all four found themselves exhausted and frustrated. The mother in-law stated that she didn't enjoy the trip and actually she never wanted to go in the first place. The daughter and the husband also express they too were not interested in going to Abilene. The father defends himself by saying he was only suggesting the trip because they were bored and they all agreed." (1)

One student interrupts, "What does this mean to us?"

The teacher replied, "The conflict they developed came from an initial general agreement. Even though no one wanted to go to Abilene, everyone had irrational fears about voicing their objection."

Another student asked, "Why?"

The teacher responded, "Possibly several reasons, but the most popular is not wanting to appear obstinate to friends, family or co-workers. Most of us wish to avoid conflict in relationships at all costs, so we suppress voicing perceived unpopular feelings and truths."

A student in the failed group replied, "That's me! I didn't agree with some of the marshmallow placements, but I didn't express my concern for fear of being viewed as not a team player." The other students in the failed group nodded with general agreement.

The teacher raised his hands as if to include all the students into the conversation and said, "So what did we learn here? We learned valuable lessons about planning the work and working the plan. We learned about teamwork and operating within time constraints.

And most importantly", the teacher was interrupted by a student, "Most importantly we learned that bad group decisions can come through the assumption of agreement."

The teacher smiled and replied, "Yep, that's the best lesson you'll ever get out of a marshmallow...class dismissed!"

Reflection:

> 1) Have you ever been worried about voicing objection in your vocation?
>
> 2) Have you suppressed your feelings in order to appear as a team player?
>
> 3) Have you experienced the Abilene Paradox in your vocation?

(1) Leigh L. Thompson, "Making the Team: A Guide for Managers," (Prentice Hall, Upper Saddle River, NJ 2000), 125.

TEN

THE ROLLERCOASTER:
Conceptual Buy-in

The front car reached the top of the climb and the coaster immediately dropped a heart-pounding 155 feet reaching a top speed of 72mph. It was two minutes and sixteen seconds of sheer adrenaline as the coaster had four loops ending in a cobra roll for the grand finale. Tom and Scott brought their families to the amusement park on a sultry Saturday afternoon. After the rollercoaster thrill, they both decided they needed a break. They grabbed some refreshments and parked their bodies in a shaded area. The collective family members agreed to return in an hour and quickly scattered to other areas of the park.

After collecting their senses, Tom and Scott broke into a conversation about work. They both held leadership positions in complementary industries, so it was easy for them to have an appreciable understanding to each other's situations. Tom shared a problem he was having with one of Tom's company's initiatives, which was implemented in the prior year.

Tom said, "We just cannot get this new workflow adopted with our national producers. We've showed them umpteen times that the initiative can increase productivity while reducing cost, yet some only partially utilize the workflow while others don't buy-in at all. The partial adoption is almost worse because it creates a duplication of effort and makes efficiencies look bad with mixed results. The others are just stubborn having more comfort in their traditional ways."

Scott chuckled and replied, "Well, we all know change is not easy...we've always adopted the adage that change is easier 'with' someone than 'to' someone. How did you roll this initiative out?"

Tom, "Oh definitely, I agree about incorporating change with the people. We thought we did a good job this time around, because we created an internal campaign and called it 'Hearts & Minds'. The concept was that we needed people to both believe it in their heart and understand it in their mind that this initiative would help us differentiate ourselves in the marketplace, while simultaneously increasing efficiencies and reducing costs. We knew that we needed both hearts and minds won over for this concept to work, because if you only believe and don't know then you cannot succeed. Visa verse, if you only know but don't believe then you will choose not to succeed. So we made sure that we won over the hearts and minds of our middle managers and they, too, became supporting voices for this initiative."

Scott nodded, scratched his chin and looked off in the distance to help formulate his response. After a few peaceful moments Scott replied, "You know, we did something like this about eighteen months ago. We broke our project down into three conceptual rollout stages: Identification, Conformity & Internalization. With Identification we reached out to strategic members of our organization to help them find commonality with what we were trying to achieve. With Conformity we used peer pressure to get resisters in-line with adopters."

Tom responded, "That sounds similar to our hearts and minds campaign just put into different terms."

Scott replied, "Ok, I'll give you that, but we took it one step further and maybe this could help you. Internalization is what's really needed. It is one thing to believe a concept in your heart and understand it in your mind. However, what really needs to happen is to put your hearts and minds to action is if the initiative is burned into your company's workflow DNA. It has to be part of who you are, what you stand for and it's like breathing...an everyday unrealized necessity."

Tom interrupted, "I hear what you are saying, but I've felt our hearts and minds campaign was to achieve what you say."

Scott smiled and replied, "Yeah, it is hard to discern the difference of going beyond understanding and believing. Think of the rollercoaster ride were just on." Tom nodded with acknowledgement and Scott continued, "during that rollercoaster ride were you thinking about anything else but the thrill of the ride?" Tom looked confused but said nothing. Scott continued, "During those turns at 70 miles an hour you were not thinking of your plans tonight or the things you need to do next week...you were at one with the rollercoaster and in the moment."

"I agree," Tom said.

Scott replied, "So, the same mind set needs to be ingrained in your people. Internalization is the next stage to take your people to get the adoption you need for your initiative."

Tom smiled and replied, "Yep, I know several who need a rollercoaster ride!"

Reflection:

> 1) How are initiatives implemented at your vocation?
>
> 2) Why can't some see value if projects carry efficiencies and cost reductions?
>
> 3) Would internalization bridge the concept gap at your vocation?

ELEVEN

THE BELL LAP:

June is the Month to Push Your Business Forward

It had been a great track season for Trevor and the grand finale, the league meet, was just in a few days. Trevor's race was the individual 800 meter, which is arguably one of the toughest races in track. A two-lap race, the half-mile is half sprint, half distance and half endurance. That's too many half's, but that is an example of how grueling the race can be. Nevertheless, Trevor wanted to run it and he had only lost once all season. Now, the league meet was on the doorstep of time and it was his opportunity to avenge his only loss.

Dad decided to walk Trevor through a race strategy that might give Trevor an advantage. Dad tapped his index finger to his lips thinking about Trevor's main competition and pondered out loud, "I wonder...hmm...I wonder if you stay within two strides of him for the first lap." Trevor nodded agreeably. Dad continued, "It would be distracting as he would hear you and be thinking about you instead of focusing on the race."

Trevor agreed with a headshake and asked, "Dad, what if I passed him on the bell lap for awhile?"

Excitedly dad agreed tapping his hand on Trevor's shoulder and replied, "Exactly, this is where we want him to think you are making your move. As the bell is rung indicating one lap left, you should thrust in front of him about three strides length. We want him to think that you are taking over the race at that point, so that he feels he needs to work hard to pass you to regain control of the race."

Trevor asked, "But when should I let him pass me back?"

Confidently, dad replied, "Let him pass you on the back stretch so that he feels he withstood your challenge. However, now he is running at a pace too aggressive to finish the race strong." Dad then stressed to Trevor, "Now on the straight-away on the backside of the track, I want you to relax and prepare for a hard kick on that last 200 meters." Dad continued, "As you approach the final curve, you bust it open giving him a sprint that he won't be able to handle."

Trevor asked, "What if I run out of gas before I reach the finish line?"

Dad shook his finger as if to brush away the air containing the worry. Dad put his hands on each of Trevor's shoulders lightly rubbing them and responded, "No worries. Remember, the action you take at the bell lap will manifest plenty of strength you need for you to finish strong...trust me."

Trevor nodded and said, "Let's do it!"

The race was as expected. What a great race and the strategy worked to near perfection yielding the gold medal.

Hours after the race, the excitement calmed. Trevor asked, "Dad, where did you come up with that strategy anyway?"

Dad chuckled because he knew Trevor would not understand. "I copied it from a situation at work", dad answered.

With a shocked look on his face, Trevor asked, "You run at work?"

By this time dad was laughing because he knew Trevor was totally confused. Dad motioned his hands to have Trevor be patient while dad explained. "I treated your two lap race like my twelve month business plan", dad said. Trevor had a blank look on his face, so dad continued, "Your bell lap represents my June. June is a great time for self-evaluating your business for successful happenings thus far in the year, how projects are progressing and for determining a forecast on how the year might end. In June, too many businesses look backwards still trying to determine how the 1st quarter resulted. By contrast, we use June to push forward on getting implemented business initiatives fully into production. Like you, Trevor, this is where I take the lead in my business race, but only for a little while. The summer months of July and August represent the back-stretch of your track where you relaxed and then your sprint in the last 150 meters is equal to my business months of September through December.

Still puzzled Trevor asked, "So why do jump out in front with your initiatives, hold back and then sprint at the end of the year?"

Dad pondered a little then replied, "June represents a key period of time for any business that is based on the fiscal calendar year. It is the last month of the second fiscal quarter and it marks the beginning of the second half of the year. Any initiative, project or sale you want to have aggressively in place by the end of June. This sets the pace for your operation on your back-stretch of the track or my third fiscal quarter. If you can get your initiatives into production in June, then they can be tweaked during the third fiscal quarter and ready for productive action in the fourth fiscal quarter as the normal course of business increases."

Trying to understand, Trevor concluded with his own words, "So the success of your June sets your business pace for the rest of the year while tiring your competitors and building your ability to sprint through the fourth quarter." Dad smiled and nodded, but Trevor continued, "So the success of your June determines if you can win the race in December right?"

Proudly, dad complemented Trevor, "Son, you get another gold medal and you see my business strategy better than most of the people I work with!"

Commentary:

New things in business are often unpredictable and risky; therefore, a pilot mode wrapped comfortably in analysis can give the appearance of progress without any true initiative advancement. June is the month to shake off the paralysis of analysis and sprint ahead with your projects if even for a short while. Once you initiate the rollout, it usually takes on a life of its own allowing you to steer the project from a leadership perspective instead of having to manage constant analysis. So do your career and your business a favor; when you hear the bell lap of June, don't deny yourself the lead. Sprinting ahead will free you from your paralysis pace and launch your project into to perpetuity of production. If you make it happen in June, then you can enjoy the sprint to the finish line in the fourth fiscal quarter.

Reflection:

1) Are you able complete and implement initiatives in the same year to help drive your vocation forward?

2) Does your organization look back or forward in June?

3) What could you do to ensure projects and initiatives implement and execute timely?

TWELVE

DAVID & GOLIATH:
Preparation

Nearly everyone knows the general story of David and Goliath. Although this story is used for religious teachings in the Jewish and Christian faiths, there are several take-a-ways that can be used for personal and business purposes. Actually, the David and Goliath story has reached people of all nations as a teaching story.

The summary of the story is as follows: David was a teenage shepherd-boy, the youngest of eight sons. He was called to bring food to some of his military brothers who were in a stand-off against the Philistine army. The champion of the Philistine warriors was Goliath, who was a giant of a man...as tall as the tallest basketball player and as big as the biggest football player. For several days Goliath had challenged the Israelites to send their own champion for a single-combat dual to decide the outcome of the war.

David hears of the challenge and asks his king if he can represent the Israelites in the dual. Who knows why the king allowed such a disadvantaged competition; however, the king at least offered his armor for some level of protection. David rejects his king's amour, but does collect five smooth stones from a nearby creek. Goliath is weighted with amour nearly from head to toe. After an exchange of a few words David uses his sling shot to score a direct hit into the slightly exposed forehead of Goliath causing him to fall lifelessly to the earth.

The groundwork was completed, David becomes famous and the future king of Israel. The story commentary focuses on David's faith as being the driving force for his victory. However, if you read the whole story you will realize that David just didn't show up as an underdog with a positive attitude. His function as shepherd-boy along with serving his family prepared him for the giant encounter.

In ancient times, the youngest had to care for the oldest. David spent most of his life serving his family's needs. This type of care prepared him for his job to shepherd sheep. Writings preceding the individual battle story details David practicing with his leather slingshot on trees and targets in preparation of protecting his flock. Additional accounts describe David encountering attacks by a bear and a lion defending his flock of sheep. The occupation of shepherd carries several hazards that require extreme preparation and a creative response to any given circumstance. David's preparation moves into the main topic of the individual battle with Goliath through collecting the five stones from a nearby creek.

There are two thoughts to David collecting five stones. Supposedly there was a rumor in the camp that Goliath had brothers, who could retaliate regardless of the terms of the single-combat dual. David may have picked up additional arsenal for that reason or he may have wanted additional stones in the event of a misfire. Either way, the written personifies preparation.

When you read on either side of the story, it is clear that David had unknowingly prepared himself for battle and victory against Goliath. Preparation is defined as to make ready or putting one's self into proper condition. (1) How many times do we fail to properly prepare for something gigantic in our business or personal lives? We should learn from David's example that advanced preparation for the known or unknown will allow us to face our personal giants. Maybe Ben Franklin says it better, "By failing to prepare, you are preparing to fail."

Reflection:

1) How many "stones" do you have ready when facing your giant?

2) How can you gain the courage to take on something giant in your vocation?

3) Do you realize you are unknowingly prepared for situations more than you think?

(1) "Preparation," Wikipedia, the free Encyclopedia, accessed July 2015 http://en.wikipedia.org/wiki/preparation

THIRTEEN

THE PARADING EL CAMINO:
Features Verses Value

It was Labor Day weekend and Shawn had lost interest in the shade-less downtown parade. It was hot, the floats were boring and no one was tossing candy. The appeal of an adjacent empty lot, a football and a few friends proved to be a force multiplier for Shawn's attention. During Shawn's departure some parade-floats, a few bands and some antique tractors paraded by. About that time some unique car noises came from off in the distance. The noise was a culmination of horn-honks and the revving of engines. It was the muscle car and antique vehicle section of the parade, which tickled the interest of Shawn.

Shawn pushed his head between dad's body and arm leaving dad's arm dangling over Shawn's body. There were all kinds of cool machines parading by: a 1965 Pontiac GTO, a 1968 red Corvette, a 1969 Chevy Camaro and a 1970 Dodge Charger all making fascinating engine noises.

Shawn tugged on dad's arm and asked in an elevated voice, "Dad, did you have one of those cars growing up?"

Dad raised his eyebrows and asked rhetorically, "These are really cool aren't they?" Then dad answered Shawn's question, "I wish I had one of those cars growing up, but they were all before my driving time." Just then a 1955 Chevrolet Bel Aire drove by with a two-tone paint job escorted by a 1959 Chevy truck.

As the cars rolled by Shawn saw one that really captured his interest. He aggressively tugged on dad's arm, pointed and screeched, "Lookie...dad, that's the same car in the picture that Uncle Bill has hanging on his wall!"

Surprised dad replied, "Yep, I can't believe you would recognize it." It was an El Camino white on the top side with maroon along the bottom. Dad stood there reflecting back to a time in the past where he was Shawn's age and rode along in the El Camino with Uncle Bill doing some farm chores.

That night dad decided to call Uncle Bill for some over-due conversation. As the two got current with events, dad decided to mention that Shawn noticed an El Camino and had the wherewithal to tie it back to Uncle Bill.

"Oh my gosh," uncle Bill chuckled. "That was a few years ago for sure," said Uncle Bill.

Dad asked inquisitively, "I remember being blown away by the half-car, half-truck concept of the El Camino...why did you get rid of it?

Uncle Bill responded, "Yeah, I remember you riding in it a few times, but honestly it was 'all hat and no cattle' for me."

Dad laughed as he was amused by the analogy and asked, "So it looked great but didn't work for you...what part didn't work?"

Uncle Bill cleared his voice and replied, "Awe, on one hand they touted it full of features, such as muscle car feel with the ability to haul cargo. On the other hand, it probably was built on a station wagon chassis as it was too low to the ground for me out in the pasture. It was rear-wheel drive so I would even spinout on taller grass because the car was light and the engine was a little bigger than average." Uncle Bill paused and then continued, "Probably the biggest factor was the price of oil in the '70's as that big engine liked to suck down the gas. Also your aunt didn't like it much as the bench seating only allowed for three to ride and one of your cousin's would be left out if we used it as the family vehicle."

Dad started laughing and remarked, "I would have liked to seen you making trips back and forth picking up family members."

Uncle Bill finished, "I did really love it and I guess now we both know that Shawn has seen the picture of it;
however, the features I was sold on originally didn't give me the value I ended up with."

Uncle Bill's comment resonated with dad and suddenly a work concept came to the forefront of his mind." Dad asked, "You have reminded me of a concept that I am dealing with at work...can you contrast a little more your comment about features you bought verses the value you got?"

Uncle Bill gave the question some serious thought as the dead air space on the phone almost became uncomfortable. Uncle Bill finally replied, "Well, at the time my business was picking up and I was gradually pulling myself out of farming. Rather than having two cars for my company and the farm, I thought the El Camino presented a one-vehicle solution. For me the value wasn't there because it wouldn't function as a truck in the field for me and I couldn't tote the family around in it on the city streets." Then Uncle Bill added, "The more I reflect, I think the El Camino experience helped me focus my business on selling value to my customers over features."

Dad asked, "Interesting, this is what we might be facing too in my company. Can you tell me how features don't transcend into value?"

Uncle Bill remarked, "Features only describe some component of what you offer in the hopes that a customer will be impressed into a purchase decision. Customers typically have a hard time connecting the 'wow' of a feature with 'how' that feature is meaningful to them. If you do make a score with feature selling then customer satisfaction is at a greater risk as the excitement of the feature will wear off and the trueness of the product or service will show through...much like my El Camino."

Dad then asked, "Then what is your version of value?"

Uncle Bill replied, "Selling value starts with the customer's end goal in mind. In the mind of the buyer, establishing value will move a purchase from a cost into a positive financial

72

investment. In short, a feature appeals to a customer's short-term 'wants' and value fulfills a customer's long-term 'need'."

Smiling on the phone, Dad thanked Uncle Bill and commented, "Here I thought I would just relive a chapter out of yester-year and actually you solved a year-long business problem for me in five minutes." Uncle Bill chuckled and replied, "Maybe you should call more often. Awe, let's just give the credit to the old El Camino."

Reflection:

1) Do the products and/or services at your vocation differentiate between features and value?

2) How can you ensure features transcend in resulting value?

3) Do you have the necessary data to ensure your products and/or services are functioning as intended?

FOURTEEN

THE BUS STOP:
Lost Sense of Purpose

Colin was a bus driver in England. The company's key measurement was the recording of actual time to scheduled time at selected stops. Colin was a below average performer and, over the course of a month, he received the necessary discipline in an attempt to lift his performance. As a result, Colin's metric began to substantially improve. His name catapulted through the employee ranking until he ranked among the top of the list of drivers. Colin became a celebrated employee and one who was dubbed with advancement potential. Colin now walked with a swagger and others marveled at his changes in himself and his success. He was on the fast track to a leadership position when the climax swiftly came about. The complaint department trended feedback on Colin's bus number and the results warranted his immediate dismissal.

How did Colin go from first to fired? To improve the metric, Colin started passing by scheduled stops with the assumption that a bus behind him would pick up the delayed passengers. Once Colin received praise, he confused the metric with his intended purpose and increased the bypassing of scheduled stops. The good metric became short-lived, though, as the repetition of missed stops angered the passengers to the point of filing multiple complaints. The metric could not supersede the authenticity of the nature of the complaints; therefore, he was terminated. Colin's defense was that other buses were on the same route so the passengers were only slightly delayed because he had been told he had his metrics to beat.

Commentary:

Colin was hired to transport people from one location to another and perform that service on a specific time frame. Colin lost his sense of purpose with his job. He morphed his serving people function into a metric result that did not correlate to his service performance. Although this story makes the loss of purpose easy to understand, there are several situations in business where it's hard to keep the core purpose of our function in focus. How do you keep yourself in focus? Be truthful in evaluation of yourself and compare your performance with regards to known company goals. Additionally, ask yourself...what I am here for and what am I supposed to be doing? Regardless of the organization, it is safe to say that you are specifically here to meet the needs of others. If you operate with that sincere premise, then you'll maintain a customer focus, which will allow you to sidestep the pitfall that drove Colin down the road to termination.

Reflection:

1) Is the core function in focus with your organization?

2) Can you sense if there is a conflict between achieving metrics and core purpose in your vocation?

3) Have you asked yourself: what am I here for and what am I supposed to be doing?

FIFTEEN

THE COMMONALITY OF THE IPHONE APP &
THE MIDDLE LINEBACKER:
Business Redundancy

It was a rough day for Bob. His youth football team had prepared all week for their game against the division rival Wildcats. Bob thought he implemented just the right adjustments to stop the Wildcat's running game. Bob has three linebackers and his two outside backers were supposed to step into the "C" gap between the tackle and the tight end to stop the effective Wildcat blast run play. In the practice scrimmages, the defensive instruction worked well building confidence for the game. The game came and went with the Wildcats clawing through Bob's specialty defense. It seems the ball carrier would cut-back into the middle of the field avoiding the linebacker covering the "C" gap hole. The Wildcats broke for chunks of yardage at a time and even scored a few times on the very play. The result was a decisive loss for Bob's team.

Bob put frustration aside and regrouped with his team during the post-game chat. As the players were dissipating, Bob reached for his I Phone to call his wife. Bob set frustration afire when the return button on his I Phone did not respond. Bob couldn't take it anymore so he tossed his phone to the ground by the ball bag and thrust his head into his hands trying to regain composure. In the distance, Coach Scott was preparing his team for play and noticed Bob's duress. Coach Scott strolled over to console Bob assuming his attitude was due to the game.

Coach Scott gave Bob a fake punch in the arm and offered, "At least it looks like the guys gave a good effort today."

Bob's eyes were throbbing with frustration and replied, "Well, my first problem is getting my stupid phone to work."

Coach Scott looked perplexed and reached down to pick up Bob's phone lying on the grass. Coach Scott asked, "What's the deal with it?"

Bob halfway pointed and mumbled, "My iPhone home button is broken and it won't allow me to reach my apps on the smart phone."

Coach Scott smiled and replied, "Actually, I think I can help you. There is a software APP that builds-in redundancy in the event the hardware breaks down." Coach Scott fiddled with the I Phone while Bob stood there half watching Coach Scott and half watching Coach Scott's team warm up. After awhile, Coach Scott handed Bob the phone back and said, "okay, look at your new 'home' APP and see if it will route you through all your options."

Bob tapped the on-screen APP button and it brought him immediately to the home screen. Bob marveled at what Coach

Scott had just done for him and eagerly replied, "This is great…thanks so much. How did you know about this redundancy with the I Phone?

"It happened to me one time and someone did the same for me so I guess I am just returning the favor," Coach Scott said with a smile. The two shook hands and started to walk away from the sideline.

Coach Scott then remembered what he was going to say. "Hey, speaking of redundancy, I was going to offer a suggestion for you for your defense."

Feeling better now, Bob chuckled, "I'll take any advice at this point."

Coach Scott waved his hands in the air as if he was on a marker-board getting ready to draw a defense. Coach Scott said, "You need to build in redundancy with your middle linebacker if you are going to plug the hole of their blast play. Bob was intently listening so Coach Scott continued, "Your middle linebacker was over running the play by side-stepping latterly and getting in the hole behind your outside linebacker. This left a cut-back seem wide open undefended, because your middle linebacker was out of position. Their coaches noticed that and abused you with that play.

Bob admitted, "Well, that is one thing I didn't notice. How do I get the middle linebacker to be redundant?"

Coach Scott replied, "By being disciplined. Your middle linebacker may not engage in the play for a tackle and may feel like he is useless. If your defensive end, your defensive tackle and your outside linebacker do their jobs then the tackle will be made. Your middle linebacker needs to control the adjacent space of the 'B' and 'A" gaps. He becomes a triangle between himself and those two gaps. Your middle linebacker is in the play only if the running back decides to cutback into the middle. In that case your middle linebacker will be there to make the tackle; otherwise, your middle linebacker is just there as a redundant safety net and essentially idle on that particular play. However, that is what redundancy is all about. Weaving back-up defenders into each play scenario so that you eventually check-mate the offense. "

Smiling, Bob replied, "So where in the world was this advice during the game? In two minutes you fixed what the Wildcats unraveled today. I have to build-in redundancy to my defense in order to stop the unplanned and uncharted situations from happening."

Coach Scott patted Bob on the shoulder and remarked, "With your good attitude and your mind loaded with redundancy opportunities, I would bet you won't loose another game this season!"

Commentary:

Typically when you hear the concept of redundancy in business it refers to a situation where an employee's job is eliminated because that employee's function is no longer needed. Another redundancy concept refers to a duplication of information technologies and data retention policies. However, one of the biggest errors any business can make is not investing in back-up processes to ensure continual operational workflows function. Resources are always tight and it is a risk to invest in redundant systems that may not be involved in generating revenue or profit especially when carrying surplus staff can be viewed as a quick way to find your business in the red.

What if the question was turned around: At what risk is your business if you don't have proper redundancy procedures in place for when the unexpected occurs? An effective business redundancy system triangulates technology with established procedure and shared resources. The Transportation Safety Administration (TSA) is an example of a redundant security program. Air travel customers are subject to identification verification at the airline ticket counter, the TSA security screening and even at the airline gate number. The whole process is a redundant chain-of-custody hand-offs double checking proper air passenger identity. The TSA partners with the airlines backing each other up to build overall confidence in the integrity of the security process. The TSA is reminiscent of the software APP for the I Phone. The APP serves as a back-up to facilitate I Phone use in the event of a hardware failure.

Part of the success of a business is how well the products and services are supported. Service shortfalls due to inexperienced employees, coupled with a continual churn of employee turnover, exposes gaps in a company's ability to sustain service continuity. Effective companies will strategically engage employee capacity to build redundant procedures in the event of unexpected changes. The middle linebacker in the story is a perfect example of this. The backer is obligated to protecting the triangle between the "A" and "B" gaps, yet serves as a redundant back-up in the event the ball carrier cuts-back unexpectedly.

If you want to take your business from surviving to thriving, then operational redundancy is the necessary investment. Planning for the unexpected should involve part technology (like the I Phone software app), part tapping employee available capacity (like the middle linebacker), and part creating a process to blend the two together.

Reflection:

1) Do you have formal back-up procedures in your vocation?

2) How does your organization handle the unexpected?

3) How does redundancy factor into your area of responsibility?

SIXTEEN

THE CAR BUYER:
Apparent Satisfaction

Paul was in the search for a certain type of used car. He monitored the online listings and perused the paper until he found an option that fit his requirements. The car was a for-sale-by-owner situation and listed at twenty thousand. This excited Paul as his budget cap was twenty-three thousand. Paul spent a few hours preparing his negotiation tactics complete with role plays and prepared a situation where he would walk away from bargaining. If the car was in good condition he would offer seventeen thousand five hundred allowing some room for negotiation.

When he arrived, he learned the car was owned by an elderly couple. Paul's generalized that that older folks drive fewer miles and give more frequent care. Sure enough, the couple had all the service records and other documents that indicated the car was in as pristine shape as it appeared. Paul wanted the car, but in a snap decision he broke from his strategy and cast a lowball offer of seventeen thousand even. The couple conferred and accepted Paul's offer. Paul was immediately dissatisfied for two reasons: He felt should have negotiated the car for less and he now worried something was wrong with the car. He was expecting some level of negotiation. Because Paul was unclear of what would achieve satisfaction, he became discontented when no price bickering occurred.

Commentary: Paul was willing to spend twenty-three thousand dollars for a car in good condition. He saved six thousand dollars and got a car in pristine condition. However, he was now unsatisfied with the purchase experience. How can someone be dissatisfied who saved thousands of dollars and increased quality in the acquisition? Paul had difficulty distinguishing satisfaction from apparent satisfaction. We define satisfaction in terms of our reactions to our events. It is possible for us to feel satisfied, without experiencing real satisfaction, if we are under the illusion of being happily fulfilled. Paul's apparent satisfaction was not met. Paul prepared for some level of negotiation and bickering. He was fully expecting that sort of buying and selling interaction to occur. When none of that occurred, Paul's satisfaction of a lower vehicle price fell prey to the emptiness of the apparent satisfaction bargaining deficit.

Paul had an internal struggle with apparent satisfaction as he could not focus on what would satisfy him. He was in search of good quality, which he found. However, then he was looking to save money, which he did. Paul lost sight of his real pursuit for happiness...finding and acquiring his unique car. All the other acquisition events got in the way because of Paul's slip into apparent satisfaction.

Ever have a customer upset with the "means" to acquire when the "end result" was just fine? It could be due to your service mistakes, or it could be due to apparent satisfaction. Here are a few things to ensure your customer transitions out of any potential apparent satisfaction. Clarify the end result to achieve true satisfaction. Define the means or disclose steps to reach true satisfaction. Finally, make your customer comfortable with the beginning-to-end process. Understanding and defining satisfaction levels should be the priority objective for those who serve the needs of others.

Reflection:

1) Can your organization help customers be clear on true satisfaction?

2) Can you think of a time your satisfaction slipped into apparent satisfaction?

3) Can you think of a way to increase satisfaction in your vocation?

SEVENTEEN

A ROSE BY ANY OTHER NAME IS REJECTED:
Code Name Naming-conventions

There is a specific dialogue in Shakespeare's play Romeo and Juliet where Juliet argues that "a rose by any other name would smell as sweet". Her point is that words or names don't change the nature of what something is; therefore, a name means less than what the "thing" really is. If Juliet's argument is in majority agreement, then why do companies pay handsomely for the derivation of a name?

We have to look no further than our own surname to understand the importance of conveying information. A surname, usually our given name, can contain details about our existence, such as origin, occupation and location. Likewise, a business name can deliver the same information. Additionally, a business naming convention can also add identity and value to the organization's core purpose. Typically business names are outsourced and carry an extreme importance, which argues against Juliet's "rose by another name" statement. Unfortunately, the chances to personally contribute naming ideas are remote; nevertheless, there are great opportunities to develop project and initiative names for your business that can enhance your company culture.

It's a delicate balance to harmonize a positive work culture amidst implementing over-arching change through new processes and initiatives. These workflow transformations already carry an emotional stigma with the dreaded word: change. These changes often require effort outside of a normal day's work duties, which manifests a physical burden to a resisting employee as well.

Often the employees impacted by the change are not included in the design of the change. Therefore, there is an inherent resistance to the initiative that pushes the change. Some project goals will carry a level of ambiguity confusing the end-user with implementation and execution of the project. Projects and initiatives often carry the notion that they are temporary so all the employee has to do is endure some strain for a little while and then the situation returns to normal. In general, people are creatures of habit so we like our routines even if they become inefficient over time. The result is a general opinion that corporate initiatives threaten our work life's contentment.

How can you, as an organizational leader, maintain culture while changing the employee misnomer of projects and initiatives? Give it a code name! Make it fun, mysterious and self-defining all wrapped in one shiny package. Just as a surname is important to an individual, and a company name is important to an organization, an initiative needs a name. An initiative with a name suddenly has a "face" with which an employee can make an emotional connection. A name gives life to a project paving the way to identity and purpose recognizable to all employees. A project name becomes the common thread of recognition from upper management to the front-line employee.

For example, a company recently incorporated an auto-dialing technology to launch an interactive voice response program for its customers. If the call recipient answered, an electronic voice would notify the call recipient that a redirect was going to occur back to a live attendant for expedited completion of some information services collected by the caller. This process is known as a "hot transfer"; therefore, in the spirit of the function of the initiative, the project was given a code name of "Jalapeño". Another example is a company who started using iPads as a collection platform for retrieving electronic data information on a mobile face-to-face basis. This was an industry first and the goal was to strategically plant a flexible device that could be leveraged for other lines of business. The code name of "Operation Johnny Appleseed" was metaphorically given to the initiative to represent a trailblazing way to bear some business fruit. Finally, a code name can also parallel with a catch-phrase. A business leader has always used the catch-phrase of "The condor flies at midnight" to tipoff the management team of impending good news for the company. Although generic, this phrase has become one with raising excitement and morale as it always precedes a significant advancement for the company.

An effective use of a code name follows a naming convention strategy similar to that as the development of a company name. There are several components factoring into name creation; however, here are four critical naming conventions pertaining to code names: memorable, visual, positive and self-defining.

Memorable & Visual: The name "Sugar Phyx" was given to a project for a company that had nothing to do with confectionery products. So, although clever, it wasn't memorable and it was difficult to spell given the play on the word "fix". A memorable code name will have a connection tethered to the attributes of the initiative. An effective code name will launch a mental visual with those who hear it. People can mentally picture a jalapeño and can easily process the concept of a jalapeño being hot to the taste. So an emotional connection can be made with the initiative of a "hot transfer" and the mental visual of the code name "Jalapeño".

Positive & Self-defining: An effective code name should sound, look and feel positive. Any corporate initiative should benefit the customer, the employee and the company. Unfortunately, there are companies who create code names for negative initiatives, such as cutting costs and reducing staff. A common saying is a cow pie that is polished to look pretty is still a cow pie. Generally, employees can see through code names that attempt to mask something that sounds good with the result that is negative for employees. While the company might have good intentions to be positive, the reverse result can occur for the employee with a lowering of morale and trust with the employer. Finally, an effective code name should be moderately self-defining to the initiative's purpose. A company gave a code name of "Schedule Now" to an initiative that allowed customers to be scheduled in an expedited manner for service completion electronically in a specific location, date and time. The initiative is certainly commensurate with the code name.

So if you are responsible for the implementation and execution of a number of these products then employing this simple tip for your projects and initiatives can help boost all-around success. A surname has an identity importance. A company name adds value importance. Finally a code name has employee emotional connection importance. At least in the business world, names can make or break the situation; therefore, Juliet's argument of a "rose by any other name" argument is rejected!

Reflection:

1) How could have a code name assisted with an initiative or project in your vocation?

2) How could you use a code name to seek support from employees who do not want to change?

3) Once a code name is created, how can the initiative or project be brought to life?

EIGHTEEN

WHACK-A-MOLE MANAGEMENT:
Time Tempts the Manager and Suppresses the Leader

Exhausted from the work day, mom slumbered through the front door into a bustling household. She couldn't even get past the foyer before she met her daughter and grandpa. "Mommy," begged her daughter, "I want to go over to Faith's house...can grandpa take me?"

Mom slipped her computer bag off her shoulder and let it slump to the floor. Just then mom noticed the cat on the kitchen counter with her son standing there petting it. Mom casted an order as if she'd said it before, "Cat...off the counter please," mom robotically commanded.

Before mom could address her daughter, dad came around the corner in a hurried fashion asking, "Where is my baseball coach's shirt?"

Already frustrated with fatigue mom looked down at her daughter and said, "No, but we will arrange for a play date tomorrow." In the same breath, mom looked at her husband and sighed, "Look in the dryer." Then mom looked at grandpa and commanded, "You can stay for dinner."

Grandpa laughed out loud and joked, "You should play that whack-a-mole game. You'd be good at it with all those decisions and instructions you just rattled off."

Knowing it was her dad; mom relaxed her stance, flipped her shoes off and replied, "Well, sometimes you just need to make decisions for people as it makes life easier on yourself."

Grandpa followed mom into the kitchen and took a seat on one of the kitchen island bar stools. Grandpa jostled the ice in his cup, cleared his voice and innocently asked, "Does this rapid-fire decision making happen at work too?"

Mom reflected for a moment and responded, "You know, lately it seems that everyone is coming to me for answers and decisions."

Grandpa asked, "Is that good or bad for you?"

Mom paused with giving the question some thought and then replied, "Both. From a management stand point, it saves time allowing my part of the company to take action sooner. There is just no time to explain or reason with people anymore, so I just make the decisions. My managers come to me with the problem and I just decide for them eliminating their chance for mistakes and reducing their delay in decision making. Just today, I must have made about five key decisions with either my managers or even their supervisors in about an hour. However, the down side is business and personal time is shrinking for me and it seems I am getting slower. I must admit I am getting tired and frustrated with the recent appearance of a growing inability to make decisions coming from my subordinates."

Grandpa joked, "You're not slow...I just saw you speedily make one decision after another like a good whack-a-mole player."

Mom asked, "I was going to ask you about that...what do you mean by whack-a-mole?"

Grandpa smiled and explained, "You know how the game is played. There are about six or seven holes where a mole will pop up for a split second and you have to take the rubber hammer and whack that mole in that split second to get points. That is a very quick decision process and sounds like a lot of what you do at work." Mom still looked a little confused so grandpa continued, "You mentioned earlier that you had to make five key decisions in a short amount of time. So keeping with our theme, you whacked a mole over there." Grandpa pointed off in the distance and then grandpa pointed in front of himself and said, "Then you have a quick decision right here and whack...another mole gone. Do you understand the analogy regarding your work problems and decisions?"

Mom looked off into another part of the kitchen amused and replied, "That does sound like me. Boy if I got a bonus for every mole I whacked in a work day, I could retire."

Grandpa laughed and remarked, "I think you could be a princess whack-a-mole manager based on the way I saw you in action when you entered the house!"

Princess is a term of endearment that grandpa called mom growing up so the reference made mom feel nostalgically good. Feeling good about her efforts, mom replied, "Well you know the old proverb…if you want something done right then do it yourself."

Grandpa suspected that type or response so he nodded to acknowledge while lifting his pointer finger and replied, "Yes, but there might be a few inherent challenges with the princess's whack-a-mole approach." Mom knew that grandpa was a seasoned veteran in business leadership so she yielded to his wisdom simply by gesturing for grandpa to continue.

Grandpa scratched his neck and then said, "Well I could be wrong but I think another old proverb works best here; give a man a fish and he eats for a day, but teach a man to fish and he eats for a lifetime." Mom started to protest, but grandpa held his hand in the air as if to let him finish. Grandpa continued, "If you start making decisions for your people, you will inadvertently condition them to defer to you on smaller and more meaningless things. In turn, this will distract you from your over-arching responsibilities while at the same time sucking your time away essentially as you have already stated. Although the pressure of time makes whack-a-mole management tempting, this makes you only a manager of task instead of a valuable leader of people. After all some of those proverbial moles you whack are your subordinates, so imagine their pain. Your people are your greatest asset and when the whack-a-mole approach is used, they essentially only represent a cost to the company. No one grows with the organization as there is no opportunity or responsibility for which to have pride. Princess, I know you too well and this whack-a-mole approach is not in your character. You have wonderful leadership qualities and I hope that you can balance management decisions with leadership teaching your men and women to fish."

Mom realized the message from grandpa and rubbed her forehead with her palm knowing that time constraints, along with other things, had let her slip into an undesirable behavior at work and home. Mom smirked and replied, "I can't believe that I am a whack-a-mole type person…ugh!"

Grandpa stood up to hug his daughter and consoled, "I have two more old proverbs for you. You are only as strong as your team's weakest link and most importantly, I'm starved…what's for dinner?"

Mom quipped back, "I think we're having the fish that you taught me to catch."

Grandpa laughed and chuckled, "Sounds better than mole meat for sure! That's my princess. I'm glad your team has their leader back!"

Reflection:

1) Can you think of a time you felt you unnecessarily needed to make a decision for a subordinate?

2) How do you balance short time constraints with the need to make multiple decisions?

3) Can you identify someone in your work life to provide you with constructive feedback?

NINETEEN

RED ROVER; SEND COLLABORATION OVER:

Execution Collaboration

In unison the group sang, "Red Rover, Red Rover send Carly right over." Carly was standing in a line of kids holding hands with about fifteen yards separating another line of kids hand-in-hand facing Carly's team. Carly shook her hands loose from the kid on either side of her and darted across the open area separating the two teams. As Carly neared the other line of kids, she instinctively slowed down causing the momentum of her body not to break the barrier of clasped hands formed by the kids of the other team. The team cheered and, since Carly couldn't break through the line, she had to stay with that team. By the rules of the game, Carly is absorbed into the other team and has to collaborate making the other team grow in strength.

In the kid's game of Red Rover, runners attempt to break the barrier of the other team's collective joined hands. The runner's strategy should be to make contact where the hands are joined as that is naturally the weakest point of the team's hands and arms' barrier. If the runner breaks the barrier then the team representing the runner gets to bring back a player from the other team. Runners who don't break the other team's barrier become a member of the other team. This activity continues until there is only one team. Red Rover is an ego boosting game for children with all kids winning as they all end up on the same side collaborating together.

Commentary:

Larger companies will offer a suite of products and services that are managed by separate teams, yet have complementary value to each other. These organizations could benefit through integrating the activities of the Red Rover game into business operation. Collaboration is a noble business concept where departments join proverbial hands working on a common purpose to achieve a business benefit. Businessdictionary.com defines collaboration as cooperative arrangement in which two or more parties (which may or may not have any previous relationship) work jointly towards a common goal. (1)

Unfortunately, there are pitfalls to inter-departmental collaboration if the intent is not properly defined, employees don't receive consistent direction and the management is not sincere. Some morph the concept of collaboration in a self-serving opportunistic way. The misuse often looks like this: One department transfers an employee and related cost to another department while assigning additional responsibility to the other department. Others don't encourage an exchange of information and the collaboration failure looks like this: Departmental management is too proud to receive outside ideas, the collaborative actions are assumed irrelevant due to the assumption the issue is too complex for outside assistance.

These non-sincere attempts at collaboration do little to unravel the silo-effect that is so common with inter-departmental coordination. The result of collaboration in these situations is essentially a waste of company resources and time. If these organizations would simply adopt the rules of the Red Rover game, collaboration could result as intended. Let's meld the Red Rover strategy with the generalized business environment. A Red Rover team, who wins a new teammate, absorbs that person as a collaborative ally. This person is committed to the new team and has valuable intelligence regarding the former team. This one-player win becomes a natural asset for utilization in the game. Couple the aforementioned with a commitment oath from management support, then collaboration is as easy as the Red Rover game. So a simple adoption of Red Rover strategy for inter-departmental collaboration can lead to the successful cooperation of team members resulting in execution collaboration.

Reflection:

1) If you joined another team to help execute on strategy, how would you ensure that your views were valuable and heard?

2) How could you help management drive the commitment of the intent of collaboration?

3) How can you make execution collaboration?

(1) http://www.dictionary.com/collaboration.aspx

TWENTY

THE COTTONWOOD SEED:
Principled Thinking

It was a beautiful day in May with a hint of summer sprayed in the air. Kevin and Darren left the breakfast area and made for the conference room at the Cherry Valley Lodge and Resort. Their parent company was holding an annual strategic meeting and they were invited to represent their respective subsidiary businesses. The conference room was just a short walk away so Kevin and Darren elected to bypass the shuttle for a stroll. As they walked, Darren said, "Breathe it in...you know this is the only peace you'll get all day long."

Kevin nodded with unfortunate agreement and added, "Yeah, none of this stuff will apply to us. They'll talk just about the core business leaving our non-essential divisions flapping in the proverbial wind."

Suddenly a car drove by causing Kevin and Darren to pause in the crosswalk before walking across a resort road. The car had the windows down and the motorist's stereo had a song blaring by a country group known as <u>Florida Georgia Line</u>. As the sound trailed the car off into the distance, Kevin's spirits were lightened.

Kevin commented, "Man, I love that song and they are my favorite group."

As they continued walking on the path, Darren pointed over his shoulder towards the direction of the car and asked, "You mean what was coming from that car?"

Kevin replied, "Yep, if only we could kick back listening to them today at this resort instead of where we're going."

Darren was more curious about Kevin's musical favorite and asked, "How can the Florida Georgia Line be your favorite group when they have released only one album with just two songs played on the radio?"

Surprised, Kevin countered with his own question, "Why don't you like them?"

Darren chuckled, "They are fine, but come-on...to be your favorite group they need to be around awhile, maybe catch a few of their concerts and have multiple songs on your iPod."

Kevin decided not to engage in debate and simply replied, "I don't know, but I love them and they are my favorite for now."

As they walked under a sizeable tree, a breeze picked up in the air causing the leaves on the tree limbs to crackle with noise. Suddenly, it started to snow white puffy-like seeds from the tree.

Kevin said, "Check that out. It's like winter." They both reached out their hands trying to catch some of the falling seeds. Darren felt some land in his head so he ran his hand through his hair.

Darren replied, "I didn't realize this was a Cottonwood Tree. Now we know why it's called Cottonwood." Kevin laughed and took a couple of swipes through the air as some of the snowy-like seeds landed on his shirt. The experience was peaceful and left them in a reverence-like state as they finished their walk to the convention center.

The convention session went long and dry, but after a break there were a series of break-out sessions with smaller groups. Kevin and Darren were assigned to the same group, as the parent company wanted to keep the non-core business units together. There was a discussion about creative ways to grow revenue and Kevin offered up suggestions that his subsidiary was doing. Darren was listening to Kevin and couldn't help but crinkle his nose at the idea. The business that Darren lead was complementary to Kevin's so Darren knew the discussion on the revenue type was clearly a departure from Kevin's company's growth strategy. Darren jotted some notes anyway and decided he would wait for a later time to challenge Kevin.

Lunch was served in an adjacent room in a round-table format. Many people wanted to hustle back to their rooms before the next session started so Kevin's table eventually became abandoned.

Darren strolled over with his dessert in hand, sat down a few chairs away and asked, "So are you really doing what you talked about back there? Darren was referring to the creative revenue idea mentioned at the earlier break out.

Kevin replied, "Sure thing and we already have sold a few of these types of opportunities."

Darren asked sincerely, "Can you reconcile these new opportunities to fit with your established directional strategy?"

Kevin looked shocked at Darren and replied, "Of course...revenue is king and that's close enough." Darren remained stone-faced so Kevin continued talking, "Those directional strategy plans were just thrown together because corporate wanted us to waste time with Marketing and PowerPoint slides."

Darren thought about how to ask nicely and then just decided to challenge Kevin. Darren asked, "I know one of those accounts and that business does not interact with your main product, your call center or even your technical team. How can you say this fits with your company strategy?"

Kevin was confused of why Darren would be so inquisitive and replied slowly to stress his point, "It's growth."

Darren sensed that Kevin was perturbed but asked anyway, "Have you talked to your operations team to see if their workflows will be close enough to churn this business to what you say is growth?"

Kevin was puzzled and asked, "Where are you going with this?"

Darren noticed a stow-away Cottonwood seed on Kevin's clothing and pointed to it. Darren said, "There you go...this is you."

Kevin sarcastically replied, "I am a Cottonwood seed."

Darren smiled and continued, "These seeds are reliant on the wind to whisk them off to a place for planting. Some fall on the road and get squished by a car. Some fall on rocks and never reach the soil. This seed found you and it thought it was a good idea, at the time, to attach to you. However, you cannot turn that seed into a tree." Kevin smiled as he was amused that Darren would give the Cottonwood seed human qualities suggesting it could think. Darren finished, "So without a real directional strategy you are like that Cottonwood seed just fluttering around looking for anything to land on in hopes that you can achieve growth." Darren stressed the word growth as Kevin sarcastically used it just moments earlier.

Kevin thought for a moment and defended himself by saying, "I don't think what I am bringing in is going to derail my company. We'll make money from it."

Darren replied, "All I asked was could you reconcile this new business to your directional strategy. I think we should go upstream from your business and establish principled thinking." Kevin's facial expression transitioned to inquiry so Darren continued, "The United States government is based on the constitution. These are a set of unchanging principles that serve as the bedrock foundation allowing for the government to set directional policy. We hear arguments almost daily that the law should be changed to promote the coolest cultural thought of the present moment. If it contradicts our constitution then the government rejects the notion, regardless of how cool it appears to be. This principled thinking is a system to guard ourselves against fads with a limited shelf life and, in general, what society may think is the right thing to do at the moment in time."

Kevin asked, "So what are some of the challenges associated with non-strategic growth?"

Thinking, Darren scratched his upper lip and replied, "Well, revenue that causes one-offs to your support network can foster inefficient service, strain the customer risking dissatisfaction and possibly even increase your costs with obviously lowering your margin. If your business lacks enough discipline to grab too many revenue opportunities landing outside your directional strategy, then you loose control of your business strategic destiny becoming much like the helpless Cottonwood seed floating at the mercy of the wind."

Kevin responded, "So you are saying I am a Cottonwood seed because my company's strategy is not principled like the constitution and I am blowing in the proverbial wind of what is popular revenue thought at the present time,"

Darren nodded yes and replied, "It is simply a matter of strategic principled thinking. It is possible for a business to float away and that is why a healthy company needs to reconcile its business ventures back to its directional strategy." Then Darren laughed and continued, "I really think you are a Cottonwood seed for saying Florida Georgia Line is your favorite band as that is the pure definition of what the country music society thinks at this moment in time!"

Commentary:

No matter where you are in your organization, you will be faced with business transactions having two-fold results: Results that benefit you and/or your area and results that benefit the organization as a whole. As a leader, your charge is to create a win plus win situation for both areas. These results are the essence of the concept of principled thinking. Do a favor for your sake of your organization's health. Conduct reconciliations on transactions that are not an obvious win plus win for you and the organization. This reconciliation can be financially based or a simple question of "how does this look and feel" can be asked to non-invested party. Do all the business deals you can, but reconcile every deal to your core strategy.

Refection:

1) How can you balance revenue opportunities with sound strategic acceptance?

2) Why is it necessary to have principled thinking with your directional strategy?

3) What would you do if your sales team sought an opportunity that didn't fit into your organization's support structure?

TWENTY ONE

THE BUFFET LINE:
Customer Care

Some time ago, my wife and I took a trip to Cancun, Mexico. We took an excursion bus to tour the wonderful Mayan ruins of Chitzen Itza. The distance was several hours so lunch was included in the excursion package. Our guide was a seasoned veteran in the tour business. He had a masterful command of weaving points of interest with amusing cultural stories that most nationalities could understand. He was a good communicator keeping us constantly informed of the upcoming events on the agenda. He truly made our excursion a memorable and joyful experience.

The best exhibit of customer care, however, was his instructions regarding lunch. Lunch consisted of a buffet with a wide selection of domestic foods and salads. Our guide set the lunch scene with detailed instructions to ensure that we ate well but didn't get delayed with other tourists. His instructions were simple. According to our schedule, we would be the first or second bus to park in front of the restaurant: however, as many as eight buses would roll in within the hour. We would be seated by bus and it was common practice to be seated first and to complete drink orders before approaching the buffet line. He advised us to avoid being lured to the table and instead proceed to the right where the line forms for the buffet. Furthermore, he suggested that we take two plates filling it with anything and everything we wanted. The reason for the two plate approach would be to avoid an unnecessary delay in line on a return buffet trip. We followed instructions and as forecasted, the dining employees were eager to fetch our drink orders when we sat down at our table with our food in hand.

Our dining experience was enhanced as we watched the scenario with other tourists and it played-out exactly as our tour guide said it would. People are typically cheerful on vacation, but a fifteen minute wait on an empty stomach can really wear on a excursionist's fun factor meter. The buses were on a schedule, which possibly created less of a tourist experience if they were not able to enjoy their lunch due to time constraints. We felt sincere gratitude for the wisdom of our guide and, of course, that manifested in a few extra pesos at tip time. Regardless if our guide's motivation was tip oriented or not, he demonstrated the pure essence of customer care.

Basic customer service would simply explain the intended flow of the lunch buffet with allowing the care part of service to be squeezed out. Customer care goes beyond service creating an emotional gratitude bond between the receiver and the giver of the service. Customer care doesn't cost extra other than just a tad bit of effort to provide your customer with an optimal experience. The "care" factor is little extra thing that makes the customer experience more enhancing and your service more differentiating.

Reflection:

1) What was your feeling the last time you received customer care vs. customer service?

2) What are the obstacles in your vocation from offering consistent customer care?

3) What one little thing could be implemented in your customer service that would enhance the customer experience?

TWENTY TWO

A CARROT, AN EGG & COFFEE:

Enhancing Your Attitude

"Dad, I don't think I can do it."

Dad, who was sitting on the couch reading, looked up and noticed a sincere look of worry on his daughter's face. Dad tried to calm her by saying, "Ah honey, it's normal to be nervous. You have been preparing and you'll do fine."

The daughter replied, "I petrified that I am going to screw it up."

Dad smiled and tried to sooth his daughter's nerves by pointing to his head and saying, "Ah honey, anything important that you do in life will be played out in your mind before any actions reach your mouth, hands and feet. The most important thing to do is develop an enhancing attitude. Once you do that you will fear nothing in life and you will enhance whatever you endeavor."

The daughter replied, "I need any help I can get so please tell me the difference between a normal attitude and an enhanced attitude."

Dad put the paper to his side, motioned to follow him to the kitchen and with a grin said, "Let me show you." Once in the kitchen dad said, "I need you to get a pot full of water and set it to boil." While action was heating up on the stove, dad rummaged through the refrigerator looking for his props. Dad found what he was looking for and partially concealed his findings as he turned towards the stove.

"What are we eating," his daughter asked with tinge of sarcasm in her voice.

Next to the stove on the counter, dad sat a carrot, an egg and a handful of coffee grinds. (1) Before his daughter could speak, he continued, "I want you to inspect each element and then place it into the boiling water. She did as instructed and they both stood in silence for a few moments watching the elements react to the boiling water. Dad took a spoon and fished the carrot and egg out of the pot and sat them on the countertop.

Dad looked at his daughter and said, "There are three types of attitude we can possess as we face challenges in our lives: soft, hard and enhancing.

The daughter lost her patience and quipped, "Dad, you could have told me that without bringing me here to the kitchen. Is there a point in all this?"

Dad felt the props had reached their purpose so he pointed to the boiling water and said, "See that? That pot represents life and the boiling water represents situations we face in life. Then dad pointed to the carrot and asked her to pick it up. She picked it up and grimaced as it started to squish in her hands. Dad chuckled and commented, "That carrot represents a hard person who encountered the boiling of life and that person came out with a soft attitude." Dad then picked up the egg and let it drop on the counter creating only a few cracks. Dad added, "Look at that. The egg represented a fragile person who experienced a boiling life and came out with a hard attitude."

The daughter interrupted, "Ok, I bet the coffee represented a person with an enhancing attitude.

Dad replied, "Absolutely, the coffee grinds represented a nervous-to-pieces person, such as yourself, but came out of life making it actually better for everyone...just smell." Dad continued, "That is my wish for you to engage in life with an enhancing attitude."

Commentary:

Your attitude touches every facet of your life. There are only two things in life you can control: your effort and your attitude. Giving your best effort in proportion to your potential is another topic, but the focus, here, is on attitude. Attitude is defined as a visible expressed behavior to a mental thought or feeling (2). Inspirational author John Maxwell says that our attitude is a choice that is individually made. You likely don't choose your situation, but like the coffee in the story, the attitudinal choice you make can enhance and influence any situation (2). An objective evaluation on the outcomes of past situations will always point to an attitude, healthy or not, that caused a choice in a good or bad action.

Choice aside, Maxwell contends there are three other truths about promoting the coffee effect of attitude over the carrot and egg effect. First, identify problem feelings about yourself. Our present attitude is a collection of feelings on past experiences, so review the areas in your life that result in feeling negative about yourself. Awareness is the start of changing your choice of attitude.

Second, identify problem feelings related to others. Personal attitude issues often result through relational experiences with others. What are those areas of challenge when dealing with others? Developing a level of emotional neutrality throughout these relational experiences allows an opportunity for an improved attitude perspective. Third, identify problem thinking. We are the sum of our thoughts so what negative thinking consistently influences our attitude resulting in an expressed behavior?

You will not be able to choose to enhance your attitude until you understand what is presently impacting your feelings and thoughts. A healthy attitude is your greatest asset in dealing with any situation, so take personal responsibility to increase awareness, develop mental area lists and consciously prepare your enhanced attitude for potential troubling situations. So remember our attitude is a choice to parallel the softness of a carrot, the hardness of an egg or the enhancing aroma of coffee.

Refection:

1) If you had to pick one element to depict your general attitude style, would it be the carrot, the egg or the coffee grinds?

2) Do you manage your business attitude differently from your personal attitude?

3) How can your attitude impact the people you lead?

(1) www.accesschristian.com. Adpated from Bits & Pieces.

(2) John C. Maxwell, "The Difference Maker," (Nelson Business Publishing, Nashville, TN 2006), 3-4, 94-95.

TWENTY THREE

GUYS:
Salutation Protocol – intent Supersedes Meaning

Upon exiting the restaurant, a woman sought the manager to express dissatisfaction with the dining experience. The quality of food was fine and the overall service was commensurate with the style of the restaurant. However, the complaint was over the salutation the "Y" generation server made to the baby-boomer generation customer and her mixed-gender party using "guys" as the greeting salutation. The woman argued, "Language matters and the server should stop using 'guys' to address mixed-gender groups". The woman went on to assert that the greeting use is a bad habit and it reminded her of her minority status in the corporate world that is predominantly male. She ended her point with expressing that she didn't care to be reminded of her frustrating professional feelings while trying to enjoy herself in a social setting. The "X" generation manager listened intently as he had recently heard a salutation complaint in a different way. The manager apologized sincerely and attempted to offer some future incentive to mitigate the present trouble with the customer experience.

As mentioned previously, the manager's dilemma was nearly the opposite just a week earlier. A complaint was lodged against the same server for referring to a female customer as "ma'am". The manager mentally retreated back to the nature of the complaint. At the time, the manager advised the server to address customers more generically. The customer perceived "ma'am" in a mockery towards age. The server adjusted the greeting to "guys" and again ended in a complaint. So now the manager has to learn to strike a balance with salutation satisfaction so that the experience can be wrapped around the service and food quality.

It goes without saying, but all business leaders have a priority to the satisfaction level experienced by the customer. In the business world, the customer is king, or in this case, queen! Each person will bring a perceptive bias to customer interaction so there is no blanket approach to a proper salutation. Moreover, we live in a day and age where there are three consumer generations with their own accepting ideas of salutation etiquette.

The reality is that generation "Y", "X" and even the baby-boomers likely reference "guys" in multi-gender greetings. The whole argument drips with irony. Some take exception to the use of "guys" as literal gender specific greeting, while others use "guys" in an attempt for a neutral politically correct safe zone. The use of "guys" is intended to refer to "all" in a greeting. It is similar to the use of mankind referring to "all" in the Bible. It is intended to avoid the confusion when there are only seconds to decide and when "ladies and gentlemen" just seem tacky or "folks" seem too folksy. People who say "guys" generally mean no harm by and are likely just using the word because it's causal and the salutation is generally accepted.

In a customer to provider relationship, the goal is to achieve a good customer experience; however, there are simply bigger battles than unintended word choice. In the end, it is not a greeting, but it is our actions of service or care that convey sincerity. In business, we need to balance the perceptive formality of language use with the sincerity of provided service.

Intended service aside, there are takeaways for improvement to ease customer perception. First, sharpen the meaning you intend and consider some customization to your salutation protocol. Predict the generation of your customer and develop a few greeting deliveries for the generations and the mixed-gender groups that are not as casual as "guys". Second, if your service and products sizzle, then there will be little discussion about salutation protocol. The intent will supersede meaning. However, responding to and debating complaints about a greeting is a sign that your service isn't where it could be. Give yourself an unbiased review (grade yourself hard) of your service delivery and make the necessary adjustments so that in the future it is known by both you and the customer that your intention is sincere and it supersedes any language meaning. That's all folks!

Reflection:

1) As a manager, how would you handle a salutation complaint?

2) How can you evaluate the intention of your service delivery?

3) How could you customize your service delivery between the three consumer generations of "Y", "X" and the baby-boomers?

TWENTY FOUR

IS THERE A GARDEN IN THESE WEEDS?:
Keeping Hubris Out of Your Leadership Garden

"Is there a garden in these weeds," questioned Joe who was standing at the back corner with his hand on his hips. Dan was pulling some weeds sitting on his knees facing the other way so he didn't notice Joe's approach to the garden. Dan didn't recognize the voice so he turned his shoulder and arched his head only to find Joe. Joe carried a nickname "Hubris Herbie", which was unknown to him, because Joe had detailed knowledge of seemingly every topic and a solution for every problem. Dan sighed inside, but appeared neighborly. Dan greeted, "Hey Joe. I've got to get caught up here don't I?" Dan and his family planted a small garden on mother's day with a combination of vegetables and flowers, but now it was weeks later and the family schedule did not allow for time for garden care. Joe repeated himself, "Yes sir. You've got to figure out if there is a garden in these weeds."

Dan hoped that Joe would realize Dan was busy and Joe would continue on his neighborhood stroll. In an attempt to end the conversation, Dan replied in a chuckle, "Yeah, I thought I would take a few minutes to police some things out here before leaving for my son's game." Most people would understand that Dan was tight with time and would leave him alone. To Joe, Dan's comment was an invitation to engage and the "Hubris Herbie" was coming out. Joe was an engineer by trade and invented some things, ran a company and actually was a pretty informed guy. Unfortunately, his personality was abrasive and his know-it-all attitude turned a lot of people sour on him...hence the nickname "Hubris Herbie".

Joe pointed and stated, "Hey, you missed pulling those weeds." Dan put his hand to the bridge of his nose in distress, but decided to humor Joe and looked to where Joe was pointing. Dan smiled and replied, "Oh, those are my hybrid tomato pepper plants. Pretty cool, huh?" Joe snapped, "No, no, those are solanum nigrom, but laymen call them black nightshades. They are weeds that produce a cherry-like fruit and spread from birds dropping the seeds elsewhere. I don't want birds spreading this over to my house." Dan stood there amazed. He had heard about some of the "Hubris Herbie" stories, but now Dan found himself directly in a clashing situation. There were four hybrid plants appropriately spaced and one of them still had a tag on it. Before Dan could reply, Joe restated, "I don't want these spreading to my yard, so I'm going to help you here." Without thinking, Dan stuck his arm like a running back stiff-arming a would-be tackler. Dan said animatedly, "Hold on." Dan paused and let his senses come back to him. Dan continued, "My kids need to be out here as this is a family project anyway. I need to leave for our game so let's wrap this up and I'll follow up with you this weekend."

Dan doesn't appear to have a proverbial "green thumb", but Joe didn't know that Dan grew up on a farm and was knowledgeable through years of experience. Likely, Joe spent five minutes in a book and deemed himself a horticultural expert. Dan could tell Joe would rather deal with the situation now rather than later. Dan walked towards Joe as he exited the garden and confirmed, "Joe, I'll get with you this weekend, but now we've got a ball game to win." As Dan walked by, he patted Joe on the shoulder and under Dan's breath he uttered, "See you later, Herbie!" Joe's mind was still processing that the dilemma would not be addressed right then so he wasn't paying attention to Dan. However, Joe was in earshot of Dan and heard something so Joe questioned innocently, "Who is Herbie?"

Commentary:

Have you ever had a five-minute conversation with a senior employee and suddenly that person was an expert in your area? Hubris is defined as having excessive pride or self-confidence. (1) In social setting, a "Hubris Herbie" is always right, a know-it-all and flourishes on the attention of being heard. The word is also a literary device used by authors and playwrights to introduce flaws with their characters. Hubris is a typical flaw in the personality of a character who enjoys a powerful position. This person overestimates personal capabilities and losses contact with reality. This character will, at times, intentionally violate moral and social codes under the pretext of righteousness. The authors and playwrights always use the hubris literary device as a tragic flaw where the character ends in defeat or rejection. Based on the interaction between Dan and Joe, the hubris literary device seems to confirm the validity of Joe's "Hubris Herbie" nickname.

In business, what does your leadership garden look like? A successful garden grows leadership plants and keeps hubris weeds in-check. Whether you are a supervisor, a middle-manager or a business leader, you have progressed to an elevated level because of your knowledge of the business and your skill-set executes well in the business.

As a leader, your behavior influences the tone for how your peers deal with you and how your subordinates operate in their own business roles. It is not easy to strike a balance between displaying confidence verses arrogance. It's even harder to look at yourself in the mirror for a sincere self-awareness review of your own "Hubris Herbie" level. Here are five tips that will help you keep your leadership garden growing without the hubris weeds:

First, humble yourself. In this sense, humility is defined as you are confident and successful but there is still much for you to learn before you think others are below your value. How to humble yourself? Be approachable at work. Walk the "floor" frequently, learn a few corny jokes, don't use big words for normal situations, eat in the workplace cafeteria and be the first to pick up any trash on the business premises. Humility is a life-long asset as it helps you place others in your mind's priority.

Second, don't let success go to your head. It is long understood that the greatest athletic coaches may not be the best coaches; however, these people surround themselves with the best coaching staffs. There has never been an "I" in the word "team" so remember where you came from prior to your success and work hard to pass your legacy of success on to others.

Third, value others. Value deeply your customers, your team, your peers and your peers' teams. You can't get everything done for your customers by yourself. Value the employees like a customer through thinking of them as your best asset and not just a necessary cost on a financial sheet.

Fourth, keep learning. Read a book, review complementary industry web case studies & find some mentors to regularly meet with. This tip isn't just to do one of the three suggestions...do them all! Learning is a constant journey and not just a graduated destination.

Fifth, communicate. Leaders of humility share information, they ask for feedback and they bring thoughts together. These actions suggest that your leadership direction is synchronized with the goals of your team. The more a leader communicates, the more understanding the team receives on clarity of objectives.

As a leader, your team and your organization needs your talents to shine. When your talents outshine your hubris, the result is a growing respect for you amongst your team and your peers. Do yourself and favor and pull the "Hubris Herbie" weed and grow the "Humility Herbie" plant!

Reflection:

1) How bad are the hubris weeds in your leadership garden?

2) How would you handle a direction interaction with a hubris Herbie?

3) Why is humility in leadership an asset?

(1) http://www.dictionary.com/hubris.aspx

TWENTY FIVE

The Ultimate Guide to the Awesome: Achieving a Work/life Balance through Body, Mind & Spirit

There is a growing feeling of angst amongst business types into today's 24/7/365 environment. Technology has gifted us with the ability to carry communications on our person anytime and anyplace. Additionally, fear has forcefully pressured business leaders to ignore the traditional confines of business conditions due to brutally clashing acquisitions, intense external competition and internal organizational resources posturing for promotions. The risk now is high when setting email to "out-of-office" because communications are virtually always available; the customer doesn't care if you are traveling for work or pleasure and someone externally or internally is willing to "do it now" the moment that you delay.

To deal with this angst, countless websites exist today to aid those in search of the elusive concept of the work/life balance nirvana. The tips for a healthy balance are plentiful whether you are categorized as an employer or an employee. The reasons are obvious as an employer: a healthy organization creates a positive atmosphere creating more employee effectiveness, which results in more customer satisfaction. As an individual, the need for work/life balance is of greater importance because the family depends on the employee's health in addition to employer. So these helpful websites shower the reader with the "why" of a work/life balance and bludgeon the reader with "how-to" tips of incremental value. Prioritizing your time, reducing valueless functions and outsourcing tasks are pieces of advice straight from Captain Obvious. These experts and pontificators are not wrong, but this collective advice merely scratches the surface of offering value to the work/life balance conundrum. A real successful work/life balance requires a subscription to the ultimate guide to the awesome.

The objective is making a better "you" out of the existing "you". In order for the ultimate guide to the awesome to work, you must understand three truths about any plan for you. First, life is fluid. Business requirements do not pause while you are out of the office and naturally your personal issues won't wait while you attend to business matters. The idea that the triad that makes up your life can be compartmentalized and separated is an idealistic leftover from a yesteryear protocol. Second, the balancing weights of work and life will vary over time. A balance does not mean equal weighting distribution between all your life's triad. There is an ebb and flow to the prioritization of your work and life responsibilities that requires you to make continuing adjustments to your life's triad. Third, any plan must be customized to your life's triad in order for you to achieve an appropriate level of success. Different people lead different lives and the website experts only toss generic tips to the masses. The ultimate guide to the awesome focuses your attention to the triad of your life: body, mind and spirit.

BODY – "body car"

Cars are fascinating machines to some. Some people will refurbish old cars; some people will keep their cars once the loan is paid off, while others will trade their cars out regularly. Associate a car with your body. There is no body trade-in process! You can do some refurbishing, but you only get one "body car". We have never lived in a time where we've had so much knowledge where nutrition, exercise and rest can impact our body cars. Equally, we have never lived in a time where there has been greater medicine and technology designed to support our body cars. Knowledge, technology and medicine present us with a tremendous opportunity to enhance the quality of our lives and extend our lifespans, just like regular tune-ups to a classic car.

When discussing the health of our body car, it is important to engage in a relational perspective. Some of our body cars are trucks that can never be refurbished into a sports car. Additionally, the importance of health just isn't limited to the coat of paint and the accessories on the body car. If the metaphor doesn't convey the point, then know this: the health of your body has to be relative to you and not be compared with those in Hollywood. Too often, the focus is on the outside appearance of the body. More importantly, the analytical function of your body's internal systems and major organs is critical for enjoying a healthy life. The diagnostics health of your body's internal systems should be in-range with the average of others in your human classification.

It seems obvious that a healthy body car would be necessary for a work/life balance, but body issues have stalled the healthcare system for decades and it has caused lost production with increased cost to employers for the same amount of time. It's simple: a reasonable diet coupled with reasonable exercise promotes better functioning of your internal systems. When you are healthier on the inside, you look better on the outside and you allow your body car to drive towards a more efficient work/life balance. Your body health is the quintessential cornerstone for the ultimate guide to the awesome.

MIND – "The precious passenger"

In continuing with the car theme, let's think of our mind as the precious passenger in our body car. The ultimate guide to the awesome focuses on two activities of the mind: input & output. Inputs are data that enters our minds and associates with our knowledge to form our thoughts. Input sources are what we read, hear, watch and those with whom we associate. The average mind is exposed to twenty-thousand messages per week, at the rate of about three-thousand per day. (1) This number is growing because of the increase of media venues as mobile technology connects people whenever they want and wherever they are. These inputs are not limited to media and technology. Every label you see has a brand message or a marketing theme designed to influence your behavior. There are so many per day, that our minds cannot absorb them all. However, people who want your influence, time and money are coming up with creative ways to connect with you. If you don't utilize some mental filter, you'll get cranium clutter where your mind becomes a proverbial leaf in the wind dancing with every wind-blowing message that inputs into your mind.

The mind inputs are pooled with our experiences and our rearing, which result in mind output. What we say and what we do is derived from input. The concept is the idiom "garbage in, garbage out". Improving the quality of mind output will enhance our work/life balance. Therefore, controlling the input is the key -but how? The ultimate guide to the awesome suggests a mind filter for your body car. Unknowingly to you, your mind is already engaged in filtering out many messages. People have different beliefs and experiences, so an unconscious mind filter is typically unique to each person. However, there are a few filters we can consciously implement to preserve the sanctity of our output from all the inputs. Here are two intentional filtering suggestions:

1) Want vs. need filter – Some wants and needs are obvious such as: I want an extra garage verses I need a retirement plan. Other wants and needs are more difficult to distinguish such as, I want to dine out vs. I need something to eat. Likely it's hard enough to discern between a want and a need, but for a work/life balance your mind filter also needs to discern between a "value want" and a "distraction want". If the "want" aligns with the normal function of your life, it doesn't

place stress with the triad of your life and it adds some level of appreciable value, than your filter worked and you are free to pursue the "value want". Otherwise, the "want" is a distraction and will subtract from your work/life balance. An example of a "value want" would be a vacation verses a "distraction want" of being sold a time-share while on that vacation, when that was never the intention.

2) Comfort zone vs. complexity filter – We are fundamentally creatures of habit where routines and repetition provide us with protective comfort when exposed to the possibility of change. However, the world is in a constant state of change and there are times when we have to let go of comfort and engage in change. The balance is to respect the intelligence of your mind in contrast to the change proposal. If the change proposal is too complex to understand the value, then the chances are greater that your comfort filter protected your work/life balance. (2)

The ultimate guide to the awesome defined some mind filters, but continuing education moves the precious passenger in your body car from neutral to driving forward. Learning never ends. It is a journey through life. If you've stopped or slowed your active learning function, then the chances are strong that your mind filter will be inconsistent. Naturally, if your mind struggles with wants, needs, comfort and complexity, than your work/life balance will be challenged. Continuing education manifests effectively in non-traditional platforms and the ultimate guide to the awesome focuses on three of these areas:

1) Mentorship – The misnomer surrounding the concept of mentoring is that the mentor is senior to the junior mentee. There is nothing wrong with this arrangement, but effective mentorships can be peer-to-peer relationships and there is a definite kinsmanship when peers are able to increase conceptual learning together. A mentorship promotes the exchange of viewpoints to a situation coming from different angles, which is known as perspective. A mentorship provides value through the exchange of experiences where situations are revealed and addressed. Furthermore, a mentorship is a proverbial petri dish allowing for simulations of proof of concepts and other ideas of creativity.

2) Relevant reading – It is not against the code of the ultimate guide to the awesome to read for pleasure. Romantic novels, sports magazines and celebrity tabloids are all forms of entertainment reading, but your precious passenger is shifted into overdrive through relevant reading. Relevant reading is simply defined as information that is directly related to or complimentary to the priorities in your life. This reading discipline deepens your understanding of your primary thoughts, it keeps focus with your life's events and it validates your mind's position regarding your priorities.

3) Peer engagement – A general macro approach to learning are cross functional exchanges through peer engagement. Spending some undivided time with the interests of people who surround you will increase your appetite for continuing education.

The precious passenger can be protected with a filtration system and can be driven through continued education. A healthy mind is a building block on the body car foundation. Together the two are nearly there for promotion of a proper work-place balance.

SPIRIT - (guiding headlights)

There is less debate over the first two triads in life: body and mind. We use our bodies and minds every day. Understanding our spiritual nature isn't as easy. Spirit is an intangible triad of life where people have the least awareness. Additionally, the word *spirit* may represent a different concept to various people. The ultimate guide to the awesome defines spirit as an impersonal life-force that brings power and guidance to our person. Spirit is the headlights guiding our body-car. Many people are uncomfortable entering into the spirit triad, especially if "work" is associated with the discussion. Remember, the environment today has fused business and personal time together; thus the need for a work/life balance. Additionally, you are the same person whether at-work or at-play. It is ironic, but the life triad needed to ensure a proper work/life balance is the one topic we most avoid in either work or life: spirit.

Be encouraged to set aside the moral compasses, that a secular society thinks is appropriate, and enjoy life at a deeper level through practicing a faith through living under those principles. We are free to choose our own belief system.

I personally believe that the ultimate guide to the awesome sources the spirit from God, who was powerful enough to create the universe, yet is delicate enough to create a personal relationship with each of us through Jesus Christ. All humans have a body and mind, which will often influence our decisions to stumble below a successful work-life balance. This is where God can tap the spirit and guide us back on track. Much of common business practice today is based on biblical principles so it does make sense to engage the spirit in the workplace. The spirit triad complements the body and mind making the work-life balance ripe for success.

Some people will disagree with Jesus Christ as the source of the spirit. That is not a problem. You do not have to believe this, but you might greatly enrich your life by exploring and developing your own spiritual nature.

We can ignore our spiritual nature or we can accept it as an important triad of life. We can worship pleasure and the world's material things or we can look for something that's ultimately more important. There is a relationship between spiritual development, character and overall well-being. The spirit is the guiding headlights in the ultimate guide to the awesome.

We live in a society that wants quick and easy answers to life's most challenging questions. Again, there are many instructional lists on the worldwide web with improvement tips to make a better work/life balance. The ultimate guide to the awesome is a sustainable blueprint that focuses on the core triads of life. Through some discipline and dedication, these triads can become parallel with health. When the body, mind and spirit triangulate, the work-life balance lifted to a new fulfilling paradigm. Subscribe to the ultimate guide to the awesome today!

Reflection:

1) What's the one thing you can do to improve the body? Get an annual blood analysis performed.

2) What's the one thing you can do to improve the mind? Set aside time in the morning to read something thought provoking and uplifting.

3) What's the one thing you can do to improve the spirit? Drop the moral compass and tether yourself to a belief system.

(1) According to Ries and Trout, in their book Positioning the Battle for Your Mind http://www.fluiddrivemedia.com/advertising/marketing-messages/

(2) http://www.businessinsider.com/planting-your-message-in-the-buzy-or-lazy-brain-to-sell-more-2013-8

TWENTY SIX

F.I.D.O.:
Dwelling on the Past

It was the last practice before the first game. The third grade football team had diligently been preparing for the upcoming season. At the conclusion of practice, the coach called all the players into the huddle along with a few by-standing parents. The coach crouched down so that he was in range of the height of the youthful players. The coach rubbed his fingers on his chin looking for the right words. "Listen up men," coach bellowed in an intentional deep voice. Coach looked around the huddle and continued, "You had a great week of training and I believe you ready for this weekend. Saturday is all about you. It is not about me or your parents. It is not about anything that happened before this game or will happen after this game. It is about you, right now, and your opportunity to play the game. On Saturday, play the way you want to play, in a way that would make you proud and in a way that would make your teammates proud. I want you to enjoy every second you have on the field and make the most out of it. I look forward to watching you compete to the best of your individual and collective abilities."

Coach paused to absorb the reactions thus far. Then coach opened his playbook binder and pulled out multiple sheets of paper. Coach distributed the papers to all the players and any leftovers were shared with the parents. Coach asked one of his players, Andy, to read what was on the paper. "Andy obliged and read big words big-font words, "Mistake, no fair and bad call." Coach looked all round letting Andy's words permeate the huddle. Coach said rhetorically, "Guess what?" He paused with his head nodding and continued, "This is going to happen Saturday." Coach repeated Andy's words rather vocally, "Mistake, no fair and bad call." Coach then repeated himself, "This is going to happen to you Saturday at some point in our game...and in other games. This is going to happen to you in the future at school. "Coach looked up smiling at the parents and continued, "This is going to happen to you throughout your lives and even as a grown up."

Coach asked, "Guess what we do about it?" Some kids shrugged their shoulders without knowing and a few raised their hands as if in class to answer the question. Coach reached out lowering the air gesturing to the players that he didn't want them to respond. Coach then handed out another piece of paper to all the players and then handed the rest to a nearby parent. The second piece of paper contained the same message but smaller in font size: mistake, no fair and bad call. Then in a huge font, the acronym FIDO appeared. About half the team had their hands raised so coach asked, "You want to know what FIDO means?" There was a collective yes as a response.

Coach decided not to wait any longer and replied, "FIDO stands for forget it; drive on." Coach paused for effect. Coach continued, "Yes, mistakes, no fair and bad calls...we are going to forget it; drive on...with every bad thing that happens. We're going to forget about the negative circumstance and we are going to drive on with a great attitude and our best effort. Here's why. When we hold onto the bad feeling associated with that circumstance, then we are focusing on the past and not ready for what comes next. When we are not ready for the next play, then we cheat ourselves with our own ability and then we hurt our team." The coach paused and then asked, "Does the need to FIDO our minds when bad things happen, make sense to you?" Collectively the team cheered with an enthusiastic yes and there were even a few parents that chimed in with cheering. As a symbolic gesture, the coach had all the players rip apart the first page of mistakes, no fair and bad call. Then all the players ceremonially threw the bits of paper into a trash can and collectively yelled FIDO; FIDO!

As the coach collected a few stray balls, a parent came up and asked, "Coach, can I have another sheet? I'm going to do this at work tomorrow with my team!"

Commentary:

Sports and work run hauntingly parallel when bad circumstances ruin your day. We're all human so it is natural to react with emotions of anger, guilt, sorrow, shame or even resentment. Fretfully obsessing about the people and events precipitating such negative feelings can lead to endless self-tormenting through reliving the past. Becoming increasingly stagnant, or fixated, with your thinking really can't progress you toward any adaptive resolution. Spending too much time on your thoughts and feelings lures you into the self-absorption mode. Once there, you lose perspective through becoming hyper sensitive to even the littlest things that don't go your way. Furthermore, dwelling on the past can become a delay tactic with dealing with today's realities. To conclude it another way, not letting go of the past will likely rob you of future opportunities that exist today within your reach.

The key is to keep rumination at a minimum. Wikipedia defines rumination as compulsively focused attention on the symptoms and causes of one's distress. The experts will advise to reconcile the cause of the problem with the feeling of the problem. Through that association, the person can make peace with the situation and close the door to the past. (1)

There is no argument with that strategy, except for that process takes precious time and there is no guarantee the result will end in peace. The FIDO method is all about time and health. Life is short, sports opportunities are few and work relations are impatient. There simply isn't time to systematically walk through our minds' cognitive hallways connecting cause with effect of the world's eventful impact on us. Furthermore, there is just too much competition everywhere so we need to keep our minds healthy with a focus of seizing the next opportunity successfully.

Forget it; drive on. That is the easiest, quickest and healthiest way to approach many of our life's challenges. In the end, it is your choice: either you can bog yourself down with self-pity, or you can FIDO yourself towards reaching your full potential. Choose FIDO!

Reflection:

1) How can dwelling on the past become unhealthy?

2) Can you think of FIDO opportunities you are dwelling on presently?

3) How could the FIDO method help you in your vocation?

(1) https://www.psychologytoday.com/blog/evolution-the-self/201108/the-past-dont-dwell-it-revision-it-part-1

TWENTY SEVEN

JONAS GRUMBY'S MISSION OF SUBMISSION:
Connective Leadership

The television show, Gilligan's Island, aired on CBS between 1965 and 1967. The show's concept was based on a three-hour boat tour in Hawaii for five individuals and two crew members. The boat was caught in a sudden storm, drifted away and the tourists ended up stranded on an uncharted island. The show's episodes focused around silly rescue attempts that were often accidently foiled by the show's feature character, Gilligan. Just watching the clumsy and befuddled Gilligan made anyone understand why the castaways remained stranded. The character Jonas Grumby (known as the Skipper), played by Alan Hale Jr., was the boat's captain as well as a central figure on the show. The Skipper, seemingly spent much of his time reprimanding the fumbling actions of the hapless, yet loveable, Gilligan. Many of the show's scenes pictured the Skipper yelling at Gilligan, whacking with his hat over Gilligan's head and even threatening Gilligan. Exploring the fan club website, one would assume to find concerning remarks about Skipper's physical and verbal disciplinary behavior towards Gilligan. On the contrary, the comments about the Skipper are noted as "caring", "selfless" and a "loveable leader".

How did the Skipper balance kindness with discipline? It could be that Jonas Grumby was intentionally casted as a character that would have the authority of a captain melded with the warm heart of a preacher. Alan Hale Jr. did a great job allowing the audience to connect with the Skipper on a personal level thereby superseding any judgment his disciplinary side. Additionally, the Skipper used a term of endearment, "little buddy" to give the audience an understanding of relationship depth between Gilligan and the Skipper. Together this on-screen charisma fostered a triangulating emotional bond between Skipper, Gilligan and the audience.

The Skipper was the leader of the castaways on and off the boat. How did the Skipper achieve this leadership designation during the melodious times of their marooned fate? Through a humbling heart, the Skipper submitted to the greater will of each castaway. The Skipper submitted to the professor's knowledge, the Howell's social status, Ginger's stardom, MaryAnn's purity and of course the Skipper submitted to the kinship bond he had with Gilligan. Ironically, the Skipper gained the respect, trust and the influence necessary to be a leader through de-prioritizing his own interests so that he could focus on the others' needs. This is a rare attribute in leadership where people sincerely admire the leader as an individual and grow in appreciation for his/her authority. People will care less about a leader's authority until they understand the leader directly cares more about their best interests.

This is the basis for connective leadership. It is generally true that effective leaders communicate well; however, television sitcoms use miscommunication as a strategy for seeking humor. On Gilligan's Island, there were several communicative mishaps, yet the Skipper is still foreseen as a wonderful leader. A connective leader influences beyond the impactful reach of a few fancy words spoken by a communicative leader. Famous author John Maxwell defines connecting as the ability to identify with people and relate to them in a way that increases your influence with them. (1) Through the art of submission, The Skipper broke the bonds of mistrust and frustration associated with being marooned on an uncharted island. The Skipper used discipline, love and accountability with Gilligan while winning the affection of the other castaways through his art of submission. The result has the Skipper modeling as an on-screen connective leader.

There are five essential attributes of submission that lend to connective leadership powers: service, applied discipline, guidance, initiative and patience.

1) Leaders share themselves and one way to share is through serving others. A serving leader brings the leader and subordinate relationship to a parallel allowing for the subordinate to develop a sincere appreciation for the leader as a person. In turn, this awards the leader an influencing authority. A serving leader views a subordinate as a human asset as opposed to an impersonal necessity. "Do as I say and not as I do" is a funny but truthful colloquialism.

The term is intended to strengthen another's discipline but acknowledges a weakness with one's self. By contrast, connective leaders need to authenticate self-discipline, but more importantly, they need to teach and apply the disciplines of success.

2) The Skipper used applied discipline to ensure that all the chores were properly allocated amongst the castaways on Gilligan's Island. This discipline created a sense of teamwork that manifested in a family-like bond as they faced the tribulations of being marooned.

3) Guidance is a key facet of connective leadership. Good leaders seek counsel regarding tough decisions and deciding strategic direction. The Skipper often sought the counsel of the professor on matters that impacted the castaway's situation. Seeking guidance actually displays a leader's strength through expressing the courage to ask. The best leaders don't know all things themselves; they gather information through inquiry, and they seek counsel from others. A better decision can be made through a collaboration of information and ideas between the connective leader and subordinates.

4) Initiative is the hands and feet to an idea. Without initiative, a leader's words lie lazily on the hammock of inaction. A connective leader has the gumption to influence others, engaging them for achievement with task oriented initiatives.

5) Finally, a connective leader needs to exude patience. The Skipper was patiently forgiving to Gilligan for often ruining rescue plans. Additionally, the Skipper was patient with developing opportunities to seek rescue from the island. A connective leader doesn't wait patiently for just anything to happen; a connective leader incorporates the aforementioned four essential attributes patiently to achieve the planned result.

Some times leaders create a sterile environment through using their positional power to simply direct others. Jonas Grumby had that positional power through his captainship, yet Jonas chose the connective leader path through submission. The result was a loving response perfectly demonstrated through the use of what others affectionately called him; not Jonas, not Sir or Captain, but Skipper. Don't let your leadership mode get stranded on the inactive hammock surrounded by the leadership storm of confusion...get your Skipper on!

Reflection:

1) How would you characterize your leadership style?

2) How important is it for a leader to seek buy-in from subordinates?

3) If employees could choose their own leader, how many would choose you?

(1) John C. Maxwell, "Everyone Communicates, Few Connect," (Nelson Business Publishing, Nashville, TN 2010), 27.

TWENTY EIGHT

DR. BONEBREAK:

When Performance Ruts feel Normal

Darren and Kim kept trying to get a dinner date with Mike and Jennifer, but their schedules were conflicting. Finally the two couples got together and during pre-dinner conversations got current with each other's lives. Kim had referred Jennifer to Dr. Bonebreak, the new local chiropractor, so Kim asked Jennifer how her back was. The ironic name for that profession caught everyone's attention and was cause for some table laughter. Jennifer acknowledged that she had seen Dr. Bonebreak a few times and commented, "Actually, I feel worse than I did before having my back adjusted."

Kim replied, "Oh my, that's not good. Why do you think that is?"

Mike interjected on behalf of Jennifer and joked, "Maybe the doctor took his name a little too seriously." Both couples chucked.

Jennifer answered, "Well, I did have a conversation with Dr. Bonebreak". Jennifer placed an emphasis on the doctor's name to add to Mike's joke, which resulted in some additional snickering at the table. Jennifer continued, "He said it was fairly common because my muscles had adjusted to my spine misalignment. My muscles were picking up the slack for my joints not working properly. The result was what was really wrong with my back began to feel normal due to my muscle compensation."

Kim repeated Jennifer's comment in the form of a question, "So what was really wrong, felt normal to you?"

Mike suggested, "Obviously not, because you had to go to the chiropractor Bonebreak guy."

Jennifer responded, "You are both right. My muscles compensated making me feel normal with what was really abnormal; however, my muscles could not sustain that normal feeling. My muscle confusion ran out causing me to see Dr. Bonebreak. "

Darren asked, "I'm confused. You said you are feeling worse than before the bonebreaker guy adjusted you." Still having fun with the doctor's name, everyone smiled.

Jennifer nodded as she gulped some of her drink and replied, "Oh yes, Dr. Bonebreak said this was common. My back was out of alignment for so long that it will take some time for my muscles to adjust back to the true normal way of my structural operation in conjunction with my spine."

Kim confirmed by saying, "So your muscles confused you thinking wrong was normal. Now your muscles are confusing you with thinking normal feels wrong."

Jennifer smiled and said, "Yes, it sounds crazy."

Mike joked, "What was wrong, you thought was normal and now what is normal really feels wrong…that is as ironic as a chiropractor with the name Bonebreak."

Kim, Jennifer and Mike were laughing at Mike's comment, but Darren had a blank stare. Kim noticed Darren's shocked look and playfully elbowed him. Kim asked, "What's the matter?"

The table laughter subsided and Darren muttered, "I have this same problem with some of my teams at work." Everyone laughed as they thought Darren was making a joke. Darren gestured with his hand as if to quiet the laughter and continued, "No, seriously. Using the same words here regarding Jennifer's back, I have some managers confusing the wrong performance as normal. Some work conditions have apparently simulated the muscle confusion thing Jennifer had and it has tricked my managers into thinking that a performance rut functions like a normal employee function.

Everyone looked confused so Kim explained for Darren and said, "He often makes bizarre parallels with life and work so here he goes again." Kim asked Darren, "Now that you've figured it out, can we get back to dinner?"

Just then, Mike raised his glass and toasted, "To Dr. Bonebreak. He's saved Jennifer's back and Darren's business!"

Everyone laughed and clanked their glasses.

Commentary:

Customers, metrics and other business conditions usually expose performance issues with employees. The performance rut is a unique condition because ruts fade into the fabric of everyday business activity and a rut's impact is usually gradual over time. Much like the confusion with Jennifer's back, a performance rut is a business process or employee behavior that is not competitive in nature to help the organization reach its goals. However, the process or behavior seems normal enough to be undetected by the manager. Humans are innate creatures of habit where people will buy the same groceries or order the same food in the same restaurants. Habit is an adversary to change so the habit stifles development creating a performance rut that feels normal to the employee. The process performance rut is often a result of an outdated workflow reinforced by the comfort of employee work habits.

What are some root causes of an employee behavior service rut? It could be boredom through the monotony of the job function, it could be burn-out with the existing job function or it could be the employee isn't the best fit for the job function. What does an employee behavior service rut look like? Metrics remain the same or fall after the employee has tried some process change. The employee is reluctant to engage areas of the business immediately outside the employee's function. The employee retracts with communication and coordination with peers and management.

Knowing when to managerially address performance ruts is an age-old business problem. Like Jennifer felt with her back, why do managers get tricked into thinking normal performance is really a performance rut? Like Dr. Bonebreak's fix, how do managers make the proper adjustments to performance ruts? The answer could be a simple shift in focus between output verses outcome, which is discussed later. However, the following three categories are some pitfalls and solutions for when performance ruts feel normal: The mirror, the hand, and the landscape.

THE MIRROR

Managers often work closely with subordinates, which will naturally tighten relationships. These bonds are normally an asset to any business as these relationships strengthen communication clarity and synergize coordination of tasks. However, the manager needs to remain objectively unbiased. Unintentionally, managers will simply get "too close" to the employee and the situation. A sign of a manager being "too close" is working for employee exceptions of grading, incentives or performance that does not reconcile to the company's goals.

Another challenge is self-reflection. Some managers feel it is a poor reflection upon themselves for an employee to have less than good performance. Typically, the manager will hire the employee so manager pride gets in the way if there is some question of employee rut performance. The manager will have a tendency to ignore or explain away the signs of performance ruts; thus, resisting any self-reflection issues.

Addressing the mirror, a manager's job is to align employee performance with company goals. The manager needs spend time directing employees towards achieving company goals and not reconciling reasons for falling short of company goals. As a leader in the company, the manager needs to understand the responsibility of leadership and that being a manager is not always a buddy relationship with employees. The manager needs to love up employees, but above all, stay true to the company mission. Most importantly, the manger needs to drop personal pride. It isn't an attack on the manger to scrutinize a manager's employee. However, it should be scrutiny on the manager who blindly defends that employee from when a performance rut feels normal.

THE HAND

Most employees have several responsibilities which are subject to evaluation, yet the manager typically will consolidate the employee's evaluation to just one score. The challenge is that an employee may be a good performer in one area, but needs developing in another area. Managers will have a tendency to allow the good performing area to supersede the area in need of improvement. Think of a hand with four fingers and a thumb. Each digit represents an area of evaluation for an employee. The thumb is larger and may be a strong area of performance. But the ring finger and the pinky may be areas where performance ruts exist. The manager overlooks the areas in need of improvement and, instead, only celebrates the performance of the thumb. The manager doesn't want to crush employee confidence so managers will accentuate the positive of the thumb. This is especially common when the company overall is experiencing good times. Ignoring issues in good times can haunt the manager when good times leave. Scrutiny is magnified in the absence of good times, so the manager is stressed now to address issues in addition to making adjustments to improve performance.

Addressing the hand, the manager has to recognize there are several areas of employee performance evaluation. The best decisions are normally made before the manager is in a crisis. Therefore, the manager needs to celebrate the positives and address the performance ruts directly and timely. The employee's confidence can remain intact with reframing the development-needed conversation. Replace "you" with "we" so now improvement becomes a team sport and not just an individual obligation. Move phrases from "you need to get better at" to "let's find specific ways to improve". Another example would be from "you are falling short on this metric" to "we haven't hit the goal yet". A manager who is not open with the employee is cheating both the employee and the company from better chances at performance. The employee is the one who can improve so give the control of knowledge to the employee. The manager needs to let the employee know the areas of good actions and areas of performance ruts.

THE LANDSCAPE

Some managers feel that they cannot address performance ruts because a unique business condition, a company internal support gap or an explainable circumstance that created the condition causing the performance rut. Some managers feel the established goal was handed down from corporate so the employee should try his/her best and the manager can explain the rest. This is a manager problem with the thought of a logical explanation to bridge the gap between what was expected and what actually happened. A manager should know there is an obligation to provide a solution in addition to reporting what happened. There is rarely a perfect business landscape so the thought of unfair business conditions is a constant. Employees are hired to overcome those conditions and managers are tasked to remove barriers to help the employees break those performance ruts.

Managers sometimes rely on the company's formal annual performance review process and, at the time of the review, the performance rut situation may not seem timely appropriate to address. Therefore, the performance rut is administratively side-stepped between the manager and the employee. The performance feedback process is fluid and not filtered only through the manager. Customers, peers and metrics all culminate providing performance feedback. An annual review is representation of past performance and a set of goals for the future. Performance ruts can be exposed and addressed if the manager would use the feedback of the employee's landscape in conjunction with the formal review process.

Addressing the landscape, the manager needs to build an understanding with employees that companies have a number of tools to combat the uncertainty of the business environment. If the employee will embrace the tools, than the chances for slipping into a performance rut become lessoned. Both the manager and employee need to understand that performance feedback is a fluid process and isn't limited to the formality of a company annual process.

Another thought about the performance rut is the concept of Output verses outcome. The concept is the linchpin that ties all three categories of the mirror, the hand and the landscape together. Output is a necessary forerunner to outcome, but output can become routine, unfulfilling and result in a loss of employee sincerity. Too much focus on output can create a normal feeling performance rut with the employee and it can trick the manager with the three aforementioned categories. Output is the effort that is made by the employee to generate an outcome. The outcome is the result what the manager seeks with connecting the actions of employees with the goals of the company. Find an employee with a normal feeling performance rut and chances are you will find a tricked manager who is too focused on the effort of output.

Output has its place in the mind of a manager, but the focus of evaluation, ranking and incentive weighting should flow towards outcome. The mirror, the hand and the landscape pitfalls will fade away with a manager transitioning focus to a results outcome. Equate Dr. Bonebreak with outcome and your employee performance ruts will start to feel abnormal to all!

Reflection:

1) Why is a performance rut bad for your business?

2) As a leader, how could you better determine if your employees are feeling normal, but in a performance rut?

3) Do you have your managerial output verses outcome traits in the proper weighting order?

TWENTY NINE

THE THREE SONS:
Know Your Audience

Three sons left home to make their fortunes and did very well. One day, the three competitive brothers got back together to discuss the problems that they were trying to fix for their elderly mother. The first said, "I built a big house for Mother." The second said, "I got her a Mercedes with a driver." "I've got you both beat," said the third. "You know how Mom enjoys the Bible and you know she cannot see very well. I sent her a brown parrot that can recite the entire Bible. It took twenty monks in a monastery twelve years to teach him. I had to pledge to contribute $100,000 a year for ten years for them to train him, but it was worth it. Mom just has to name the chapter with verse and the parrot will recite it."

Soon thereafter, their mother sent out her letters of thanks. To the first son, she wrote, "Trevor, the house you built is so huge. I live in only one room, but I have to clean the whole house." To the second son, she wrote, "Shane, I am too old to travel, I stay home all the time, so I never use the Mercedes and the driver is rude anyway. To the third son, her message was softer, "Dearest Andrew, you were the only son to have the good sense to know what your mother likes...thanks for the Bible and the chicken was delicious!" (1)

Commentary:

The humorous story illustrates what can happen when we don't do something as obvious as asking what one likes, wants or needs. All three sons had good intentions for their mother and spent excessive resources to create, what they thought, were good solutions. The problem that often arises, however, is when we decide to put our own thinking in the place of others' thoughts. "Knowing your audience" is a business commandment when selling to and servicing on behalf of a customer. In the story, the three sons were trying to provide a solution to problems their mother didn't even have. Additionally, the three sons actually create a problem through failing to understand their mother or at least what their mother's needs might be.

We should not pretend we know what's best for someone or assume someone feels the way we do without first seeking to understand through inquiry. How? Listen to understand what someone is saying verses preparing your response while someone is talking. When you ask for an individual's likes, wants and needs, you message to the person that you care. Establishing care lays the groundwork for trust, which will lead to a mutual understanding. This connection now allows you to "know your audience", which influences selling decisions and better aligns service with expectations.

To avoid "the three sons" syndrome...know your audience!

Reflection:

1) When servicing customers likes, wants and needs, make sure you don't put yourself in place of the customer.

2) What can help you better understand a customer's needs?

3) What can help you prevent "the three sons" syndrome?

(1) John C. Maxwell, "Winning with People," (Nelson Business Publishing, Nashville, TN 2004), 71-72.

THIRTY

"ISH":

It takes Accuracy & Precision in Your Business

Mark concluded his report with some metrics and some financial results. Mark asked for questions. Tom was jotting some notes on a loose piece of paper. He lifted his pen towards Mark's way as a signal to ask a question. Mark nodded to Tom and lifted his eyebrows as if to receive his question. Tom asked, "Would you call this project successful?"

Mark smirked with a nod and replied, "Successful-ish."

Tom grimaced in an understanding way and scratched his chin allowing him time to choose his words. Tom then showed some mercy and joked, "That's a good one. We spent the whole front part of this meeting promising to work towards precision with our data, decisions and results and you toss out an 'ish'." Tom finished, "That's a good one."

Mark understood that he was being challenged and back-peddled verbally, "Well we were precise, but our accuracy was off target, which resulted in the watering-down effect with our success."

Tom was confused and asked, "Aren't the two terms, accuracy & precision interchangeable?"

Mark shook his head no slowly thinking of an example. Mark answered, "It would seem that way, but the two terms are different in one way and are complimentary in another way. Accuracy measures the difference between the actual result and the goal, while precision focuses on how close multiple actual results are to each other."

Tom looked confused as if the conversation topic had changed. Mark snickered and explained, "Think of a dartboard. Accuracy is how many times the bull's-eye is hit and precision is how close the darts are from each other. The goal for success would be to have the darts in the bull's-eye and the darts are literally on top of each other."

Mark noticed that most understood the explanation. Mark sighed and continued, "So with regards to our project, our metaphorical darts were close to each other but our darts didn't hit the bull's-eye. So we were successful-ish."

Tom nodded with appreciation and responded, "I had not thought of those terms in association with a dartboard so thank you for the illustration."

Tom added, "This is actually a step in our necessary direction. Today, no one is asking for 'ish'. Anyone can check on smart-phone data usages as we sit here in this room. We can know how many people web-search our name daily. The information available today is apparently so precise and accurate, that the experts tossed Pluto out of the solar system. Those examples just scratch the surface of the information available at our fingertips. As Mark said, our 'darts' need to not only hit the bull's-eye, but they also need to land on top of each other."

Tom concluded, "Let's leave 'ish' alive and well for our competitors to play with!"

Commentary:

"Ish" is a suffix that makes any word or phrase vague. In the story "ish" is used as a stand-in for "sort-of" and kind-of". The suffix is often used in situations to avoid getting mired in details during more topical and general discussions. Unfortunately, the use of "ish" has extrapolated itself incorrectly and finds its way into the business world in a damaging way. Over time, "ish" becomes close enough allowing for vagueness to penetrate our specific goals. It's a perfect dichotomy of terms when business goes with "ish" while customers want accuracy and precision otherwise.

Here are two ways to snuff-out the "ish" for accuracy & precision: communication and data. Communication clarity is likely the most important key to improving accuracy and precision. Use names instead of pronouns. In the story above, "he" could refer to either Tom or Mark. Make it clear to the reader to whom is referenced. Use titles instead of nouns. Instead of saying you read a book, say the book title. Start conversations with backgrounds of the topic and use specific information with examples.

The second tip moves available information to actionable data. A spreadsheet full of data with multiple columns and thousands or rows is a document full of information. There is a belief that once a spreadsheet is opened, an hour of productive time is lost through sorting tables and other pivots to get information to speak. Find a way to get the information moved to data that prompts decisions and actions. Employing these two tips into your business model will most certainly help you remove "ish".

Refection:

1) Where is "ish" allowed in your vocation?
2) Can you think of areas where accuracy and precision are not in harmony?
3) What can you do to minimize "ish" in your own functions?

THIRTY ONE

THE NON-INDIFFERENT RATTLER:
Appreciating & using Customer Feedback

"Indifferent," Matt blurted out in a gasp as if he was asking a question. This was in response to Betsy asking Matt how things were going.

Betsy was perplexed so she inquired with a chuckle in her voice, "What do you mean?"

Matt took a deep breath and calmly, but dejectedly, replied, "In a call earlier today, my top and most tenured customer used indifferent as the one word to describe our service delivery."

Betsy raised her eyebrows and consoled, "Ouch! Maybe that conversation somehow can be turned into strengthening your relationship with that customer. Betsy continued, "Either way, you will have a nice, relaxing eighteen holes to mentally work on it."

Matt had agreed to be in Betsy's cart for a charity golf scramble. Over the years, Betsy had been an effective mentor to Matt and he suddenly saw an opportunity get a few free hours of counsel to address his dilemma with his customer.

Betsy and Matt reached golf-hole number seven, which was a long par five with a pond blocking the fairway two-thirds of the way to the green.

Matt had been unusually quiet so, as they pulled the cart up to the tee-box, Betsy tried to refocus Matt on having some golf fun. Betsy grabbed her smart-phone and asked Siri, "What's the definition of indifferent?"

Siri immediately replied in the recognizable voice, "Indifferent means, having no particular interest or sympathy; unconcerned." (1)

Betsy smiled at Matt and advised, "Okay, so I need you to be non-indifferent here." She paused to see if Matt caught that she was playing on the word indifferent. Matt caught it and was listening to Betsy, so she continued, "You are great off the tee-box and, if you are not careful, your driver will drop the ball right into the pond. We need you to leave your drive short of the pond so that we can have a chance to reach the green in two strokes. Then Betsy grinned and joked, "It's why I have you here!"

Matt smiled, and acknowledged her attempt at situational humor by simply replying, "Funny."

However, it worked and Matt decided to have a little fun on the golf course. Just as Betsy requested, Matt shortened his drive and left the ball short of the bank of the pond near some rocks.

Betsy laughed, "Now you're in the swing of things!"

Matt replied, "Pun intended; I'm sure."

The two parked the golf-cart, grabbed their clubs and chatted as they strolled down to the pond's edge. Betsy dropped her ball next to Matt's as she would swing first. Betsy had a nice swing onto the green and then made way for Matt. Matt's position to strike the ball found him closer to the rocks.

Suddenly, they both heard the distinctive sound of a rattle. Anyone living in the Midwest knows that unmistakable sound of a rattle from a rattlesnake. Betsy noticed the rattler camouflaged and coiled between two rocks and began to point. Matt didn't wait for Betsy to message and started to jog away donating the golf ball to the snake. Even though they were at a safe distance, they continued to hustle back to the refuge of the golf-cart.

Sitting in the cart, Matt turned to Betsy and gasped, "Well there's some excitement for the day."

Betsy nodded in agreement and added, "That rattle certainly got my attention."

They decided to use Betsy's ball and replayed their snake experience as they drove the cart across the pond's bridge over to the green. After successfully completing the hole, Betsy started relating the rattler to Matt's business situation.

Once in the cart, Betsy inquisitively asked, "Aren't you glad the rattler was non-indifferent?"

Matt chuckled with wonder and in a laughing voice asked, "What do you mean?"

Betsy referred back to Siri's definition of indifferent and retorted, "The snake...the snake could have had no particular interest or sympathy. The snake could have chosen not to communicate, let you get too close and then you could have ended up snake-bit." Matt knew he was getting some free counsel so he listened intently for Betsy's message. Betsy continued, "So our rattler friend cared enough about the situation." Betsy paused and restated, "Cared enough about you to warn you that there was a problem. In return you did something about it to the satisfaction of both you and the snake."

Matt nodded in agreement and responded, "It's like I got a free gift today, didn't I?"

Betsy retorted, "No, you got two free gifts today."

Matt was confused and questioned, "Huh?"

Betsy patted Matt on the shoulder and concluded, "The snake was the second free gift. Your first was your customer who called you indifferent...that was a rattle. Aren't you glad your customer is non-indifferent?"

Commentary: Through the discussion with his customer, Matt received a free gift; however, Matt let his emotions supersede the value of the word indifferent used to describe Matt's service. A great business leader can discern the usual customer rhetoric of wanting things perfect, faster and cheaper from the warning rattle of a non-indifferent customer. When customers choose your service, you become part of the same team. The customer wants you to succeed so that the customer can flourish. So someone like Matt should embrace the customer feedback of indifferent as non-indifferent from a caring team member who happens to be a customer. This is an opportunity for improvement. Unfortunately, most customer rattles are confused or dismissed due to the assumption that customers don't understand the inherent challenges of the provider's service or product delivery model. The result is nothing happens and the provider gets fired, eventually, through the indifference of the customer over time. The customer might stay, but feels disenchanted and now the relationship is snake-bit. The customers who stay will feel "stuck" because of all the investments made initially to choose the provider, coupled with, the worry that transitioning to another provider will be too disruptive for changing. So the customer stays but feels like a business hostage. The relationship will sour as the customer's expectations will morph and the provider will become defensive leaving a snake-bit relationship.

There are three simple things a provider like Matt can do to detect the value of customer non-indifferent feedback: Scorecard, expectation setting & sprint-goals.

Scorecard – With the access we have to technology and social media, we live in a time where much can be known about service or product delivery almost immediately. The provider should steer the customer to creating a scorecard with objective metrics for defining the path for successful teamwork. Remember, the customer chooses the provider so the two parties are now together as one team. The creation of this scorecard will naturally spur some transparency between the provider's delivery model and the customer's desires. This scorecard can be established to capture objective results for an appropriate time period. The objectivity of the scorecard helps keep subjective emotions from hi-jacking the status of the relationship. There is a common saying that a provider is only as good as the last service or product, which carries a large connotation that emotions will overrule facts if allowed. The scorecard will help balance of objectivity with subjectivity in a business relationship, which in turn will allow a provider like Matt to discern the feedback of non-indifferent customers.

Expectation setting – Sales representatives typically view this as a threat to continuing customer relations. The average representative would typically rather battle internal departments of the provider as opposed to agitate the customer's disposition on attempting to steer what the customer wants. However, if the scorecard is developed in harmony with the customer, then the proverbial heavy lifting of setting expectations is already completed. When a highly charged situation occurs, the team (both the provider and the customer) can bounce the situation off the scorecard to understand if the relationship is off course. The team can also determine if adjustments are needed to the scorecard. Either way, expectations of a customer are now established to minimize highly charged situations from impacting the overall relationship and perception of service.

Sprint-goals – When humans are involved there are always challenges with subjectivity of opinion or perception. An objective scorecard will not fully define a relationship between the customer and provider; thus, sprint-goals can be used to infuse some subjective balancing with the objectivity of just data and metrics. Small tweaks with workflows or manageable changes to technology are examples of sprint-goals. These are adjustments along-the-way with the relationship between the customer and the provider. These adjustments will help keep the scorecard relevant and, at the same time, maintain expectation setting. Sprint goals are created in unison with the team and give the customer a feeling of reasonable control in the relationship.

The objective of implementing a scorecard, expectation setting and sprint goals creates an agreed and visual environment of where service stands in the relationship. Once this is created, then a provider like Matt can easily appreciate the rattle of a customer's non-indifferent feedback.

Reflection:

1) How could you better appreciate the rattle of a complaining customer?

2) How could you steer your present customer relationships towards the creation of an objective scorecard, expectations and sprint-goals team approach to service challenges?

3) How can you discern the difference between customer rhetoric complaining and customer non-indifference feedback?

(1) Reference to Siri; the built-in intelligent assistant with the iPhone.

THIRTY TWO

MISS THE ELEVATOR AND YOU SUFFER STAIRS:

A Two Minute Message to Define Your Purpose

"I realize that my closing comments are between lunch and your stomach," remarked the speaker. A portion of the group chuckled anxiously as the time was well past due according to the agenda. The crowd's applause escorted the speaker off the stage. The chief executive officer (CEO) regained command of the room through providing a number of instructional adjustments to the agenda. The group would reconvene in just forty-five minutes placing a significant constraint on the lunch line and inserting a bottleneck on the bathroom.

Drew was a lower level director representing his non-core business unit at the annual corporate meeting. Drew didn't have the best connection with many of the attendees so he decided to sit at a table by himself checking a few messages with one hand on his smart-phone and the other hand on his fork. After a few moments, the room was filled with the bustling of foot traffic and the buzz of indistinct chatter of a few hundred people. Drew was lost in his own world catching-up on email when a voice startled him, "May I set with you?"

As Drew angled his head upward, he was surprised to see the CEO with a plate full of food. Awkwardly, Drew partially stood as a symbol of etiquette inviting the CEO to the table.

"Please do," Drew exclaimed in a nervous, crackling voice. Drew introduced himself and his role in the smaller non-core division of the company. The two exchanged pleasantries regarding the amenities of the facility and how good it was to get everyone together for a few days.

After a time, the CEO innocently asked, "So how are things in your world?"

Although Drew was nervous, it was exciting for him to hear this question as his company had just experienced their best monthly financial performance. Drew responded that October was the busy season in Drew's industry and the company was able to capitalize on the additional volume through maintaining service levels despite the larger volumes.

The CEO qualified his question, "How is your company able to do better when the conditions of the market place and the economy are working against all businesses?"

Drew thought for a second and responded, "We've been innovating with our service model with the use of an iPad."

The CEO was finished with his lunch and felt the need to move on so he congratulated Drew and excused himself from the table. Drew reflected for a moment and his smile soon turned to a look of regret. Drew told the CEO that a piece of technology, which any other company could replicate, was the very thing that made his company so special during torrid times. Drew had not strategically prepared his mind for a conversation about the mission and purpose of his organization. Instead, he blurted out the first thing that came to his mind, an iPad technology, which was an important initiative; however, it did not represent the company's proverbial secret sauce. Drew watched the CEO continually move through the crowd meeting and greeting people until he slipped out of Drew's sight. Maybe it was a coincidence or maybe it was just Drew relaxing; however, as soon as the CEO disappeared, the whole message hit Drew. Drew scrambled to prepare his smart-phone for drafting this key message.

Drew addressed the email to all of his direct reports and entitled it "miss the elevator and you suffer stairs" as a symbol of the opportunity he just missed with the proverbial elevator speech to the CEO. The email had three areas of focus: Family, culture of cause and eye on the customer.

1) Family - many of our employees are not just assets...they are family so we do a little better to watch each other's backs while also holding ourselves a little more accountable. We celebrate, we encourage and we produce.

2) Culture of cause - Enough of us have connected with a deeper purpose then just some strategic vision. Our cause was to create a better industry solution that would deepen customer relationships through unparalleled speed, a relentless attitude and detailed execution.

3) Eye on the customer - Enough of us are disciplined to deploy and execute tactics that focus on the customer's positive experience resulting from our service.

In just a few moments, Drew had poured his heart into the email. He pushed send on the email and felt a sense of fulfillment wash through him. In an indirect way, the conference had been a complete success for Drew. He was connected with his company's deeper purpose before, but now this conference prepared him to verbalize it quickly. Drew noted that he had just enough time to freshen up in his room before the afternoon agenda started. The elevator doors were open and inside stood the chief financial officer (CFO). Drew entered the elevator and introduced himself and his role in the organization. As the doors closed, the CFO innocently asked, "So how are things in your world?" Drew pressed his floor number on the elevator console and had a grin from ear to ear!

Commentary:

Every business in every industry has numerous battles that distract, delay or even prevent a company from rising above the others. The above concepts are intangible and "up-stream" from the daily grind we experience in business. These concepts don't permeate throughout the organization overnight. They are not concepts sitting on a list waiting on a leader to go through the motions checking them off and then expecting a better cultural environment. These concepts ripen overtime and are rooted in ways that connect people with purpose. If done properly, a company's purpose can move people from a simple job to a fulfilling cause. Stories that build legends, promotion of unique customer relationships and process advances that expose value are the keys to building something special. It is less about the technological gadgets (as those often are copied by competitors) and more about the cultural virus that infuses the entire organization uniting around a cause. Causes launch crusades and crusades connect enough of the people with their purpose. The result is always a special environment where people don't just work...they love what they do.

The above is a strong argument and, although true, no one seems to have the time to hear that message. The solution is to create the "elevator speech". Think of this as a commercial about you and your company's purpose. The elevator speech communicates who you are, what your company's mission is and what makes you, with your company, special. Tactics and details are confusing and time consuming; therefore, the elevator speech focuses on the objective soul of the company, with its purpose, and not so much the tactics. The message should be limited to less than two minutes, depending on the audience. Miss the elevator and you suffer stairs!

Reflection:

1) Can you think of a time you missed on opportunity to give a key message?

2) Who would be your targets for an elevator speech?

3) Can you distinguish between your strategy and the cause of your company's purpose?

THIRTY THREE

GOTTA CROSS THE MISSISSIPPI IN MINNESOTA:
Break Problems into Manageable Pieces

Eric asked his dad and uncle to step into the living room as Eric needed some advice. Eric said, "Uncle Charlie, Can you help me? I've got a big problem at work that involves multiple departments, covering several states and various people."

Looking away from his nephew Eric, Charlie stated in a low but confident tone, "Well, you gotta cross the Mississippi in Minnesota."

Thinking he didn't hear what uncle Charlie said, Eric shook his head as if he had a clogged ear and asked, "Uh, Uncle Charlie, why are you talking about crossing a river?"

Eric's dad also shook his head and added with a smirk, "Yeah, Chuck, I am missing the leap of topics from Eric's problem to your river crossing."

Uncle Charlie repeated, "I've done it before. Lake Itasca in Minnesota is the head waters of what becomes of the great Mississippi river. I've walked across the Mississippi in Minnesota."

Intending to end this part of the conversation, Eric sarcastically retorted, "Well, most people cross rivers in boats or they drive across bridges."

Eric started to leave the room hastily but Uncle Charlie had more to comment. Dad tried to balance allowing Charlie to speak with acknowledging Eric's frustration. As Eric scurried by, Dad reached out and softly grabbed Eric's arm and pulled Eric into dad's chest for a man-hug.

Uncle Charlie was looking out the window and added, "Too many people try to cross the Mississippi and can't swim against the heavy current. They get frustrated and never reach the other side's riverbank. As for me, I cross the Mississippi at Lake Itasca where it's narrow with stones and people can walk across barely getting their feet wet."

Eric motioned with his head for dad to follow him. Dad winked back and followed Eric's footsteps into the kitchen.

Dad leaned against the counter and opened his hands as if to soften Eric's demeanor.

Eric quipped, "Okay, so I've had enough of the Louis and Clark river exploration. I've got a real problem and I thought I might be able to get some adult advice."

Dad chuckled and replied, "I have to admit, I thought your uncle was completely off-base but, after thinking it through, he is on target." Eric began to position his body to object but dad interrupted, "Now wait a second and let your Uncle's point soak in. He is talking about taking your problem and breaking into smaller workable parts. Uncle Charlie's lowest common denominator is where a person can walk across the Mississippi...in Minnesota."

Eric was patient and acknowledged, "Okay, I am not sure the Mississippi is the best metaphor but I understand breaking up the issue into manageable pieces."

There was a noise and both looked through the kitchen doorway noting that Uncle Charlie was swiping at the window with his hand.

Dad looked at Eric and in defense of Charlie said, "You see son, you just need to hang in there with Uncle Charlie's concepts and after a while you see just how smart he is."

Eric concentrated on what Uncle Charlie was doing and then replied back to dad with a snide remark, "Oh yeah? So if Uncle Charlie is so smart then why is he swatting at flies that are on the outside of the window?!"

 Commentary: You've probably heard it before: The simplest explanation is usually the correct one. Detectives use this approach when trying to solve crimes...elementary, my dear Watson. Doctors use it to determine the illnesses behind the symptoms...tell me what you are taking and I will tell you what you've got. Uncle Charlie was talking about a line of simplistic reasoning known as Occam's razor, which simply means to slice through a problem or situation and eliminate unnecessary details. (1)

The name stems from William of Occam who lived in thirteenth century England as a monk and philosopher. There are two principles to the concept: the principle of plurality, which means that plurality, should not be advanced unless it is necessary. The principle of parsimony, which means it is pointless to do with more, what can be done with less. Both of these principles support that simple explanations come from evidence that we already know to be true.

The more we allow a problem to grow with complexity; we allow emotion to creep into the issue along with a gradual loss of focus. No wonder we, as humans, struggle to resolve issues because we convince ourselves there is too much involved for us to wrap our heads around and solve. However, we commonly believe that the quickest way between point A and point B is a straight line. Keeping it simple, Uncle Charlie uses the metaphor as an easy, objective and less emotional way to address problems. Occam's razor also agrees that you gotta cross the Mississippi in Minnesota.

Reflection:

1) Can you think of a past problem that could have been broken into pieces that would have been easier to resolve?

2) How could you employ Occam's razor into your problem solving tools?

3) How does simplicity help solve problems?

(1) www.science.howstuffworks.com/occams-razor.htm

THIRTY FOUR

MERCURY MIKE & THE QUEST FOR THE THERMOSTAT
Pressure Leadership Styles

Sam sighed, "What? Another emergency meeting scheduled? There he goes again."

Kim sarcastically inquired, "Did someone have a grammar issue in an email again?"

They both chuckled. Sam clarified, "I was in a meeting earlier today and I think this time the emergency is about us falling short on budget."

Kim gasped, "This is like a broken record. We are coming off our best financial year, including a near match on budget. Unfortunately, this month is traditionally slow for our industry and it just happened to be more sluggish than usual for us. The same thing happened last year and it was treated as an unnecessary crisis. How do we go from superstars to falling stars in such a short time frame?"

Sam nodded in agreement and added, "In all fairness, I think there are three areas that create these emergency situations. First, corporate doesn't know our side of the business as well so they rely more on financials to judge our value and success. Second, the budget alone doesn't umbrella our investments, our value and goodwill presence we experience in our industry. Lastly is Mercury Mike."

Kim interrupted, "Yeah, I have often heard the nickname of Mercury Mike."

Sam continued, "Yeah, mercury is that quicksilver watery substance that works in a thermometer. Mike is the bridge from corporate to us and he feels he needs to function as a thermometer telling us what the temperature is. Instead, his ideal leadership function would be that of a thermostat, where he should tell us what the temperature needs to be." Sam concluded, "So Mercury Mike feels he needs to reflect the temperature of the situation, whether coming from corporate, a customer or other."

Sam's comments glued together a better perspective for Kim. She started thinking and replied, "I think the temperature gauge thing is an excellent analogy. I am still a little fuzzy on the thermometer verses the thermostat though."

Sam responded, "Mercury Mike has been in this mode for a while, so the temperature concept has emerged as a leadership analogy over time." Sam tapped his chin with his index finger as he organized his thoughts and then continued, "A thermometer reflects the temperature of the environment. It simply reacts to what's happening around it and has only one purpose to tell how hot or cold it is. Conversely, the thermostat regulates the environment. It proactively works to maintain the temperature within a range. It is intelligent. It sets the temperature range, decides when to act and it works to correct the temperature up or down." (1)

Kim was nodding in agreement and excited to add to Sam's comments, "Oh let me guess. Thermometer leaders intentionally, or even unintentionally, proverbially stoke the fire when tension gets high and people are on edge. These leaders may desire to do right; however, they usually only increase the stress level everywhere."

Sam was grinning as Kim finished and added, "Or the thermometer leader loses perceived sincerity in messaging and people stop listening or deeply discount the severity of the message."

Kim replied, "And that is exactly where we are now with Mercury Mike." Kim thought and then asked, "So we know what a thermostat leader is but how does such a leader do it?"

Sam replied, "It has to be the exact opposite of what you just said about how the thermometer leader does it."

Kim then thought out loud, "Okay, so when a company is hot under a heavy workload, burning resources are scarce or the ashes of a budget is missed; thermostat leaders will cool things off by acting as a calming influence. They align emotion with the troops through listening and then they set a rallying course through removing barriers. Most importantly they follow up with a vote-of-confidence after every tough 'why' or 'how' question."

Sam said, "That's perfect and don't forget that thermostat leaders toss in some lighthearted fun by setting goals and then celebrating with rewards albeit possibly small."

Kim responded, "Yeah and when all that happens, the thermostat leader is rewarded with the trust and confidence of all the company's people."

Sam commented, "Unfortunately, Mercury Mike is headed for eroding trust and confidence much like what we feel at this moment."

Kim agreed but retorted, "Mike is a good guy and corporate has him as our leader. We should take him to lunch and talk with him."

Sam asked, "What would we tell him?"

Kim replied, "Just the same as what you told me. What the difference is between the thermometer and the thermostat."

Reflection:

1) How would you characterize your leadership type: thermometer or thermostat?

2) Why do some leaders choose the thermometer?

3) What is one thing that you could change to lean you more permanently towards the thermostat?

(1) leadingwithtrust.com/2013/areyouathermometerleader

THIRTY FIVE

"THE ONE THING":
Develop an Adherence Strategy

In the movie City Slickers, a group of friends from the city takes a vacation at a dude ranch. Curly, played by the late Jack Palance, is a hard, crusty old cowboy full of wisdom. He gives some great advice to Mitch, played by Billy Crystal, who is facing some mid-life questions. Here is the scene:

Curley: You all come out here about the same age. Same problems. Spend fifty weeks a year getting knots in your rope – then you think two weeks up here will untie them for you. None of you get it. Do you know what the secret of life is?

Mitch: No, what?

Curley: This (holds up his index finger).

Mitch: Your finger?

Curley: One thing. Just one thing. You stick to that and everything else don't mean [anything].

Mitch: That's great, but what's the one thing?

Curley: That's what you've got to figure out. (1)

Great scene...great advice. Leaders have to figure out the "one thing" that defines a meaningful purpose for their companies.

A strong relationship between a company's strategy and an adherence to that company's strategy will set the foundation for the "one thing". Four company adherence traits support the "one thing" approach.

1) Roles are clearly defined for executive, managers and employees

2) Business needs and visions are communicated deep into the organization

3) Performance measurements are continuous and aligned with the strategy

4) Leaders are held accountable

There are enemies to maintaining adherence to the strategy that reaches your "one thing". A company may be able to set and implement the plan, but be aware of the degradation of focus that the "noise of the day" will suck away. Little by little quick fixes are installed to regain directional composure, but this inconsistent adherence sets the plan adrift. Another pitfall is overlooking blind spots. The greatest liability is the one unknown. A blind spot is any situation where our perception about ourselves and/or our function is different from reality. Most business types have personal and professional blind spots. Plans lose adherence when efforts fall short with blind spots. Lastly, negative assumptions are an adherence deterrent. Henry Ford once said, "Whether you think you can or you can't, you're right". As a leader, your assumptions have a significant and lasting impact on your team. Your assumptions affect your responses to other people and situations. Your responses, in turn, directly influence others' reactions to you. When team members observe your behavior, they begin to create their own assumptions about you. These assumptions drive their responses to you, and a reinforcing cycle develops. This cycle forms the limits, either high or low, of your team's adherence traits. Negative assumptions kill adherence to the "one thing".

What's the "one thing"? Know your costs! In sales, knowing your costs will help you set a competitive sales price. In operations, knowing your costs will help establish effective workflows. In finance, knowing your costs will accelerate a strong return on investments. Knowing your costs will free-up your business to pursue the company's strategy using the adherence traits. Not knowing costs will set the plan adrift and create adherence pitfalls. Tell Curley we've figured it out...cost knowing is the "one thing!"

Reflection:
1) Can you think of another "one thing" more important than knowing your costs?
2) Can you identify things that do not support the "one thing"?
3) Can you implement adherence traits to support knowing your costs?

(1) Lee J. Colon, "Sticking To It," (Cornerstone Leadership Institute, Dallas, TX 2003), 12.

1   **Iridescent Myopia:**

Keeping Objectivity with a Customer's Personal Color-bias

She is red hot. He is green with envy. She's a yellow coward. He's singing the blues. They are white with delight and the company is in the black. Color is an inseparable part of our everyday lives and its presence is evident in everything we perceive. Everyone chooses a favorite color and that choice is based on a personal bias of the chooser. Many of us feel strongly about our favorite color as it provides us with a familiar comfort bonding us emotionally. Our bias, our "color-bias", stems from our individual psychological make-ups and how we use our biased judgment to relate to situations.

Since it is part of our psyche, this same color-bias accompanies us into the business world. Our activities, our judgments and our interactions are based on the same bias that attracts our favorite color. The trouble that arises is that business people will confuse the mission of determining what's best for the company with the introspective thinking of, "How do I feel about this?" If business needs and personal desires are not synchronized, then suddenly the product or service is less about performance and more about the color-bias of the customer's feelings. When these situations occur, customer feedback can be "great" one day and "sucks" the next day. For customers who have individual biases supersede all else, this makes product and service improvement initiatives into a moving target. The individual customer's bias is business myopia. This is a short-sighted and heavily inward looking approach focusing on the individual's color-bias and not the needs of the company. The solution is to add "iridescence" to the individual's color-bias.

Iridescence is a phenomenon of certain surfaces appearing to change color depending on the angle of view or the change in light. A providing company with a color-biased customer must get the customer to view situations from a different angle or in a different lighting situation. The iridescence will mitigate the color-biased myopia allowing the business relationship to return back to a partnership. Here are two ways to get iridescent myopia to reposition your color-biased customers: 1) create a charter of product or service expectations using team members from both the provider company and the customer company. This way, one individual from the customer company cannot insert a color-bias that will warp the relationship. 2) Always compare results and situations to the created charter so that there is a systematic comparison free of emotions stemming from a color-bias.

2   Tootsie Pop's Indian Wrapper:

Small Encouragement can make the Difference

How many licks does it take to get to the tootsie roll center of a tootsie pop? If you watched the television commercial in the 1970's, you would know that Mr. Owl answered the boy's question with three licks and one chomp. Tootsie pops are heartwarming to kids young and old. There is even a legend association with the chewy-centered lollypop: The legend of the Indian wrapper. The Indian figure wears a headdress and is arching a bow with an arrow pointing towards a star. Reportedly, the Indian figure appears on one-third of the tootsie pop wrappers and legend says that an Indian wrapper can be returned to the company in exchange for a free tootsie pop.

Although the ability to exchange the Indian wrapper for a fresh tootsie pop is a busted myth, there is a certain encouraging pleasure when a wrapper reveals our Indian friend. Because it is not present on all the wrappers, the Indian parallels the small encouragement of a fortune cookie. In the end, it really only takes a small thing or two that can make an encouraging difference.

How can the Indian wrapper help you encourage others throughout a business day? Send someone a text of appreciation on their phone. Send someone a simple email that you heard something good about someone. Take a few seconds and actually send a small card with nice sentiments. Thank you tootsie pop for the small encouragement of our Indian friend!

3   The Wing-man:

Humility through Flexibility

In 1986, Paramount pictures launched a blockbuster film called Top Gun. One of the underlying themes was not the main character, played by Tom Cruise, Maverick's participation in the Top Gun competition...rather an inner battle with himself trying to overcome his mysterious relationship with his deceased father. He had to deal with the terms of how his father's military status and reputation was viewed. Through that conflict, his conduct displayed some inflexible and arrogant behaviors. One example would be his refusal to respect rules and authority. His cavalier attitude caused him to break a fundamental flight rule of "staying with your wing-man". The wing-man was a back-up and support role concept where the wing-man protected the primary fighter from side and rear attacks. Maverick would not settle for a support role.

Through a series of downfalls, Maverick finally learns the truth surrounding his father's situation and he has the courage to come to terms with his own reality. At that point Maverick humbles himself to follow the situational protocol of becoming the wing-man during a real combat situation. Through denying himself, Maverick ironically ends as the movie's hero. It is an example that we can achieve our goals through these unusual means through embodying the integral traits of humility through flexibility!

4   It's My Call:

Decision Ownership

In 1995, Universal Pictures launched Apollo 13, which was an awesome film based on a true story involving the ill-fated moon landing mission. Astronauts Lovell, Haise and Swigert were scheduled to fly Apollo 14, but are moved up to 13. It's 1970, and America had already achieved its lunar landing goal, so there was little interest in this routine flight until things went very wrong. Aside from the mid-flight spacecraft malfunction, there was drama shortly before take-off. Astronaut Mattingly was the original pilot teaming with Lovell and Haise. Mattingly was exposed to the chicken pox virus, without immunity, and the NASA administration gave Lovell, the mission's captain, two choices: stand down for a later mission or accept Swigert as the back-up pilot.

The next scene begins with the emotional reaction of Mattingly based on Lovell's decision. Obviously, Lovell opted for Swigert as the pilot, which created a highly charged moment of tension for the Apollo 13 team. Both Haise and Mattingly assumed the directive came from the bosses so they pressed Lovell for crafting an argument to the front office. While it was true that the NASA admin bosses dictated the situation, they did leave the final decision to Lovell. Lovell responded to the objections of Haise and Mattingly in this way, "It's my call." Lovell expressed a decision ownership that all employers desire from their leaders. Lovell could have easily commiserated with Haise and Mattingly and deceptively participated in a retort; however, Lovell claimed ownership for his decision through saying, "It's my call."

Unfortunately, there is a trend today for leaders to attempt skirting hard choices through name dropping decisions on a higher level. Simply put, leaders who do that give away their power and authority. A company doesn't need leaders to claim they are only proxy to a tough decision coming from someone else. There are leaders who will respect their own authority and take ownership of these tough decisions. Those Lovell-like leaders will be the ones whose careers launch like a rocket. It comes down to decision ownership. Own your leadership responsibility with company decisions...especially the Lovell-like calls!

5 A Little Lagniappe from N'awlins:

Discretionary Energy

Pronounced "lan-yap", the word and concept originated in New Orleans. In the eighteenth century, the area was booming with French, new Americans and Spanish settlers. The concept was used as a differentiating tool for merchants and street vendors to influence customer buying behaviors and garner purchasing loyalty. Lagniappe is a small gift or a small addition to the purchased volume as a gesture of goodwill. A customer buying twelve doughnuts and receiving the thirteenth for free or buying something advertised on television and receiving a second for free are examples of modern day lagniappe concepts. This concept is timeless and has no cultural boundaries.

How could you incorporate some lagniappe qualities into your own interpersonal skills? The answer is to unleash your discretionary energy in the workplace. Discretionary energy is simple: It is the little extra effort made where an employee goes beyond the call of duty to complete a task or to produce a result that is a little more than what was expected. The amount of lagniappe an employee will give at work is in direct relation to employee satisfaction and perceived employee opportunity. Even if there is no culture or celebration in your workplace for going over-and-beyond with effort, there is an opportunity for you to showcase your talents through the lagniappe with your discretionary energy.

As a leader, you want all employees to release their discretionary energy at work to improve their individual performance and, as a result, improve company performance. The last thing you want is for an employee to do exactly what you tell them to do with nothing more involved. Employee lagniappe is a company's fuel for moving a competitive advantage to a decisive advantage. Leaders lead by example so discretionary energy at work begins with you. Go get a little lagniappe from N'awlins!

6   Green Food Coloring:
Motivational Spirit

It was St. Patrick's Day in Marshall. Doug and Grant were financial auditors working on assignment in one of the town's factories. The two decided to pay a visit to the local watering hole for dinner and partake in a little Paddy's day celebration. The waitress brought a couple of draft beers and some festive food. Grant noted the bartender was using an eyedropper placing something into the beer cans for the guys sitting at the bar. Upon inquiry, they learned that the eyedropper contained green food coloring and the guys were celebrating drinking green beer. Doug noted that these guys could not actually see the green beer they were drinking as they were drinking from cans and the beer color was actually pointless. Doug and Gant laughed hard thinking it was ridiculous to drink green beer from a visually concealing can.

The waitress overheard the two and came over to help. She said, "True motivational spirit doesn't appear to the eye, it is generated from the heart. Those guys at the bar don't care that they can't see green. Their motivation to celebrate comes from the spirit within." It was actually Doug and Grant who now felt ridiculous. Grant asked, "Can I have the green eyedropper in my draft?" Doug added, "I'll take my spirit in a can!"

7 The Girl:

Facing Your Giants

High school wrestling is an amazing thing to watch. Weight classes keep competitors in appropriate proportion for matches. However, the similarities end there as wrestling is a grueling test of individual strength, technique and mental toughness. There is no bigger concern in high school wrestling than the female wrestler. There is usually a reason why they are wrestling, whether it is quality experience or unique skills. There is no upside for a boy to wrestle a girl. If the boy wins there is no pride gained in beating a girl. If the girl wins there is much pride lost for the boy.

Travis was a freshman who had wrestled his way into a varsity spot late in the season. Through individual meets, he had been scheduled to wrestle three girls and he forfeited all three matches with the reasoning that it wasn't appropriate to wrestle a girl. The league meet was a team scoring event and, sure enough, there was a girl in Travis' weight class. The girl's school mascot was the Giants. Travis' record was two wins to one loss when he was scheduled to wrestle the undefeated girl. Travis sat by dad to inform him that he was going to forfeit as usual to the girl. Dad asked Travis to place his team's interests in a priority over his own. Dad asked Travis to examine fully his own psyche and to be truthful of what the real issue is with the girl.

Travis was truthful and revealed that his reluctance was a fear of losing or not wrestling well against the girl. Dad told Travis, the issue wasn't about the girl at all. It was about Travis' mind and the lack of respect he was giving himself for preparation, speed and internal drive that he developed throughout the wrestling season. Dad told Travis that fear is a force multiplier and sooner or later we all have to face fighting our Giants. Dad concluded, it was time for Travis to give himself some credit for his work and preparation. It was time to face his giant. Travis beat two Giants that day. What giants do you avoid facing?

8 Never Give Up:

Persistence with Passion will often Win

A frog was hopping around a farmyard, when it decided to investigate the barn. Being somewhat careless, and maybe a little too curious, he ended up falling into a pail half-filled with fresh milk. As he swam about attempting to reach the top of the pail, he found that the sides of the pail were too high and steep to reach. He tried to stretch his back legs to push off the bottom of the pail but found it too deep. But this frog was determined not to give up, and he continued to struggle. He kicked and squirmed and kicked and squirmed, until at last, all his churning about in the milk had turned the milk into a big hunk of butter. The butter was now solid enough for him to climb onto and get out of the pail!

The story is an extreme example as it suggests passionate persistence or face certain death. However, think of yourself for a moment. You are an amazing story of persistence and you don't even know it. As a baby you crawled and through persistence you walked. That same type of illustration manifested in different ways countless times through your timeline of childhood to adult status. Your passion to do something coupled with your don't-give-up attitude and you were successful. This persistence was inherent to you.

In business there are so many times where we forget our persistent nature and we give-in on achieving something as it seems success is too elusive. People give up far too quickly on goals and dreams that are, in fact, achievable through passionate persistence. Very often, people give up just when they are on the verge of success. So when facing tough situations do yourself a favor and turn the trouble into butter!

9 Tight End OR the Line

Accepting where You can Contribute the Most

Marty had a great high school career as a tight end. He had the perfect physical tools at six foot five in height with above average foot speed. His dream was realized when his favorite

NCAA state college recruited him to play football. The spring season going into his sophomore year, Marty was third on the depth chart at the tight end position. Marty was certain he could get a greater notice at the upcoming spring intra-squad scrimmage. Shortly before the scrimmage day, coach called Marty into the office. Coach predicted that Marty would have a strong contribution to the team sooner than later; however, it would require transitioning his position from tight end to a lineman. Marty rejected the idea so coach asked him to think about it further.

The spring intra-squad scrimmage was played and Marty found himself on the sidelines not reaching the field of play even once. Subsequently, Marty fell to fifth on the depth chart at the tight end position and he didn't realize there were that many tight ends on the team. After some soul-searching Marty realized that football was a team sport and he wanted to find a way to play. He asked the coach if the offer was still on the table. Upon graduating, Marty was a three year starter at a the right tackle position and achieved all-conference honors two of his three starting years.

Marty learned a valuable team lesson that it was beyond his wishes and knowledge to know where Marty's best contributing value was. Only when he placed the best interests of the team over his own desires, did Marty excel. Although initially painfully frustrating, Marty eventually understood and accepted his role where he could contribute best.

10 Acronyms:

Messages from M.O.M.

A mom recently texted her three sons some sentiments of encouragement. She wanted to make sure they had it for when they did need it. She wrote in acronyms:

- If you FAIL, never give up because F.A.I.L. means "First Attempt In Learning.
- The END is not the end. In fact, E.N.D. means "Effort Never Dies".
- If you go NO as an answer, remember N.O. means "Next Opportunity"
- Love M.O.M. which means Must Obey Me!!!